LAY SAINTS
Martyrs

LAY SAINTS
Martyrs

JOAN CARROLL CRUZ

TAN Books
Charlotte, North Carolina

Cover design by David Ferris.
www.davidferrisdesign.com

Cover image: *Triumph of Faith - Christian Martyrs in the Time of Nero*, 65 AD (oil on canvas), Thirion, Eugene Romain (1839-1910) / Private Collection / Photo © Bonhams, London, UK / Bridgeman Images

Cataloging-in-Publication data on file with the Library of Congress.

ISBN: 978-0-89555-848-0

Printed and bound in India

TAN Books
Charlotte, North Carolina
www.TANBooks.com
2016

This book is
dedicated with love
to
The Holy Family

CONTENTS

CONTENTS

CONTENTS

AUTHOR'S NOTE

A NATIONAL Catholic magazine polled a thousand of its readers to learn what they believe about the saints. The magazine reported that while news reports on the nation's Catholics have highlighted disagreements with traditional Church teachings, sixty-seven percent of the survey's respondents said they prayed to the saints as much, or more, than they did years ago. Sixty-eight percent of the respondents said they tried to imitate the lives of the saints.

Mentioned as the four favorite saints were the Blessed Mother, St. Joseph, St. Francis of Assisi and St. Thérèse of Lisieux (the Little Flower). With the exception of the Blessed Mother and St. Joseph, who are in a unique category, we are left with a Franciscan brother and a Discalced Carmelite cloistered nun. While we can admire the virtues of St. Francis and St. Thérèse, the lifestyles of these two saints, and other saints of religious orders, are far removed, to say the least, from those of secular people.

Although the exact number of canonized saints is unknown, we know, of course, that the greater majority have been members of religious orders. We love them, we admire them, we wish to imitate them, but how can a mother with small children, a wife with a difficult husband, a young bride with in-law problems—how can they really relate to the nun who lived in the quiet of a cloister, the nun who lived in a community where everyone shared the work of the house? How can they relate to the saints of religious orders whose lives were arranged in an orderly manner and who had designated times for quiet prayer and who had little or no financial problems? One might wonder if these saints of the cloister would have merited their titles if they had remained in the world to face the conflicts and dangers confronted by ordinary lay people.

It is profitable, of course, for laymen to love these saints, to pray to them and to imitate their virtues as much as they are able. But it seems that laymen would draw more encouragement to advance in prayer and virtue and would derive more consolation in their trials by examining the troubles and temptations of those saints who lived and died as secular members of the Church.

St. Teresa of Avila suggests that "we need to cultivate and think upon, and seek the companionship of those saints who, though living on earth like ourselves, have accomplished such great deeds for God." Here, then, are the lives of secular saints who have, so to speak, "lived on earth like ourselves." Represented here are single men and women, mothers and fathers, soldiers and servants, doctors and lawyers, the humble and the noble—all who have met the difficulties and challenges of the secular life and triumphed over them. Their virtues are to be admired, but most of all imitated. May we benefit from their example and from their prayers.

—Joan Carroll Cruz

PREFACE

A WORD ABOUT THE
BLESSED VIRGIN MARY

A BOOK about secular saints would be incomplete without mentioning the pre-eminent model for secular people, the Blessed Mother. But what could be said here that has not been mentioned about her already in numerous biographies and devotional works? We have only to delve into these to find a solicitous and understanding mother, a kindly and generous friend, a consoling companion, and a ready and willing intercessor with God.

Although it is known that Mary was free from sin, full of grace, blessed among women and the fairest honor of our race, yet, as we know, she was not exempt from countless trials and hardships. She, who was the model of saints throughout the ages, should be the particular ideal of secular people, since Mary was an exemplary member of our secular ranks. She was, of course, a young bride, a young mother, a housekeeper, a widow. . . .

May this Immaculate Mother pray for us, that in our imitation of the Saints, we can advance in virtue and eventually join her and her sainted children in our heavenly homeland.

LAY SAINTS
Martyrs

And when he had opened the fifth seal, I saw under the altar the souls of them that were slain for the word of God, and for the testimony which they held. And they cried with a loud voice, saying: How long, O Lord (holy and true) dost thou not judge and revenge our blood on them that dwell on the earth? And white robes were given to every one of them one; and it was said to them, that they should rest for a little time, till their fellow servants, and their brethren, who are to be slain, even as they, should be filled up.

—Revelation 6:9–11

ONE

BLESSED ADRIAN FORTESCUE

D. 1539

SIR Adrian Fortescue was born in 1476 to an old Devonshire family which traced its ancestry to the time of the Norman Conquest. His father, Sir John, held important posts at court; his mother was Alice Boleyn, a cousin of Anne Boleyn, whose marriage to King Henry VIII was to bring about the fall of the Catholic religion in England—as well as the martyrdom of countless Catholics.

Sir Adrian's early and middle life was that of a typical country gentleman of the time. He was a serious, thrifty man, careful in business, exact in accounts and a lover of the homely wit of the day. Because his family fortunes had been secured in earlier times, he was also a man of considerable wealth. He was a justice of the peace for the county of Oxford and assisted at the royal court. In 1513 he fought in France at the Battle of the Spurs, and in 1520 he was in Queen Catherine's train when she went to Calais during the Field of the Cloth of Gold. Always a religious man, Sir Adrian was admitted in 1532 as a knight of devotion of St. John of Jerusalem (the Knights of Malta). The following year he was enrolled at Oxford as a tertiary in the Third Order of St. Dominic.

Sir Adrian was also a married man and the father of two daughters by his first wife, Anne Stoner. Twelve years after her death, he married Anne Rede of Boarstall, who bore him three sons.

During the time that King Henry VIII was persecuting Catholics as a result of his differences with the Pope concerning his marriage to Anne Boleyn, Sir Adrian seems to have behaved with prudence. But for reasons that have not been given he was arrested on August 29, 1534 and detained in the Marshalsea prison. He was probably released in the spring of 1535, the year during which St. Thomas More and St. John Fisher were beheaded for the Faith for refusing to side with King Henry VIII in the matter of his divorce and remarriage. Because Catholics and priests were being arrested for their faith, Sir Adrian, well-known as a Catholic, must have expected the inevitable. During February of 1539, the expected occurred when he was arrested and sent to the Tower of London.

Parliament met in April, and Sir Adrian was condemned without a trial. It was claimed that he "not only most traitorously refused his duty of allegiance, which he ought to bear to Your Highness, but also hath committed divers and sundry detestable and abominable treasons, and put sedition in your realm." The nature of these treasons was never given. Condemned at the same time were Cardinal Pole and several others because they "adhered themselves to the Bishop of Rome." Catholic tradition has always held that Sir Adrian died for the same cause.

Bl. Adrian was beheaded with Bl. Thomas Dingley at Tower Hill on July 8, 1539. Since his death, his cultus has always flourished among the Knights of St. John. He was beatified by Pope Leo XIII in 1895.

In the church at Husband's Bosworth is preserved Bl. Adrian's *Book of Hours*. On the flyleaf he had written and signed a series of maxims, or rules, of the spiritual life. A few of these are the following:

> Above all things, love God with thy heart.
>
> Desire His honour more than the health of thine own soul.
>
> Take heed with all diligence to purge and cleanse thy mind with oft confession, and raise thy desire or lust from earthly things.
>
> Resort to God every hour.
>
> Be pitiful unto poor folk and help them to thy power, for there you shall greatly please God.
>
> In prosperity be meek of heart, and in adversity patient.
>
> And pray continually to God that you may do all that is His pleasure.
>
> If by chance you fall into sin, despair not; and if you keep these precepts, the Holy Ghost will strengthen thee in all other things necessary, and this doing you shall be with Christ in Heaven, to whom be given laud, praise and honour everlasting.
>
> (Signed) Adrian Fortescue

TWO

SAINT AFRA

D. 304

IN HER native city of Augsburg, Bavaria (located in southern West Germany), Afra was a well-known prostitute. Her three servants, Digna, Eunomia and Eutropia, were also well-known for their disorderly lives.

However, when the persecution of Diocletian threatened, St. Narcissus, the holy bishop of Gerona, was driven from his see and for a time lodged in the home of Afra's mother, Hilaria. During his stay he converted not only the mother, but Afra and her servants as well.

Realizing the gravity and the number of her sins, Afra became a sincere penitent and wept bitterly for the pain her sins had caused her Redeemer. She did all she could to make amends for them by giving what she had to the poor and by spending time in fervent prayer and penance.

When the citizens of Augsburg noticed the conversion and Afra's new occupation of aiding the poor, she came under suspicion of being a Christian when the persecution of Diocletian reached the city. She was arrested and brought to trial before a judge named Gaius, who knew of her former life of sin. He ordered her to sacrifice to the gods, to which Afra replied, "I was a great sinner before God; but I will not add new crimes, nor do what you command me."

Gaius then revealed that he knew Afra had been a prostitute, and he promised that her paramours would return and make her wealthy if she would only sacrifice to the gods. This and other offers were all rejected. Threats of torture were dismissed with the words, "Let this, my body, which has been the instrument of so many sins, undergo every torment; but let my soul not be contaminated by sacrificing to demons."

Gaius passed the sentence of death by fire. Executioners seized Afra, carried her to an island in the river Lech, and tied her to a stake. The prayer that Afra offered just prior to her death concluded with the words, "By this fire, which is about to burn my body, deliver my soul from everlasting flames." The executioners then heaped a pile of dry vine branches about her and set them on fire. While Afra was still praying, the smoke billowed up and suffocated her.

Standing on the opposite side of the river during the martyrdom were Afra's faithful servants, who had followed her in the ways of sin and later had joined their mistress in her conversion to the Faith. When the executioners left, the three women went to the island—and with the martyr's mother, Hilaria, and some priests, they carried the body to the family's sepulchre, which was located two miles from the city.

Fleury, a church historian, informs us that the sepulchres of the ancients were often buildings large enough to contain rooms. While Hilaria and her company were in the sepulchre preparing to entomb Afra's body, Gaius was informed of what was taking place. He immediately dispatched soldiers with an order to demand the mourners to sacrifice to the gods or face death. When the soldiers could not persuade the group to comply, they filled the sepulchre with dry wood, thorns and vine branches, set fire to them, secured the door and left. In this way St. Afra, her mother and the three servants all died of suffocation and merited the crown of martyrdom on the same day.

In writing about St. Afra, St. Alphonsus de Liguori relates that we are grateful to such respected church historians as Fleury, Orsi and Massini for preserving the details of the martyr's life. St. Alphonsus also writes that

> Penitent sinners may receive great encouragement from the consideration of the fortitude communicated to this penitent by the Lord, which enabled her to suffer martyrdom of fire; and also from the consideration of the wisdom given to her, by which she answered the insidious arguments that were intended to pervert her.

St. Afra, St. Hilaria and their three sainted companions are inscribed in the *Roman Martyrology* under the date of August 12. It has been firmly established that St. Afra, who died in 304, was venerated from the earliest times. This fact is also proved by Venantius Fortunatus, bishop of Poitiers, who mentions St. Afra in his poem dedicated to St. Martin, which was written in the sixth century.

The remains of St. Afra rest at Augsburg in the Church of Sts. Ulrich and Afra, where she continues to be venerated.

THREE

SAINTS AGAPE, CHIONIA, AND IRENE

D. 304

DURING the persecution that raged against the Church
at the beginning of the fourth century, the citizens of
Thessalonica (now northern Greece) were asked to prove their
rejection of the Christian faith by eating meat that had been
sacrificed to the gods. One day when Dulcitius, the governor,
was hearing the charges against certain Christians, his secretary, Artemesius, began to read a report that had been sub-
mitted by a public informer. The document read as follows:

> The pensioner Cassander to Dulcitius, Governor of
> Macedonia, greeting. I send to Your Highness six Christian
> women and one man who have refused to eat meat sacrificed
> to the gods. Their names are Agape, Chionia, Irene, Casia,
> Philippa, Eutychia, and the man is called Agatho.

Unknown to the informer, he could have lodged another
complaint against three of the women, who happened to be
sisters: Agape, Chionia and Irene. According to a decree issued
by Emperor Diocletian, it was an offense punishable by death
to possess or retain any portion of the Sacred Scriptures. Even
their parents were unaware that the three sisters had portions

of the sacred books which they studied in secret whenever time permitted.

Dulcitius asked the six women and one man standing before him, "Why will you not eat of the meat offered to the gods, like other subjects?" To this and other persistent questions, the three sisters, as well as the others, repeatedly answered that they could not cooperate because they were Christians and that they would rather die than offend the true God.

Among other questions, there was one asked of all who were taken captive: "Have you books, papers, or writings relating to the religion of the impious Christians?" Agape and Chionia answered that they did have these forbidden papers, which they considered to be a treasure of great value. The sentence of Dulcitius came swiftly and angrily: "I condemn Agape and Chionia to be burnt alive for having, out of malice and obstinacy, acted in contravention of the divine edicts of our lords, the emperors and Caesars."

Irene was sent back to prison, but after the martyrdom of her elder sisters she was again presented to Dulcitius, who ordered her to reveal the names of the persons who had encouraged her to hide the papers relating to the doctrines of Jesus Christ. Irene's only answer was that Almighty God had commanded them to love Him unto death and that she would prefer to be burned alive rather than surrender the Holy Scriptures and betray the interests of God.

After declaring that neither her parents nor the servants nor the neighbors knew of the hidden Scriptures, Irene was given a sentence more cruel than the one given to her sisters. For refusing to relinquish the sacred books which she loved, it was ordered that she be stripped and exposed in an immoral house. When she was miraculously protected from abuse, she was martyred. One source claims that she was burned at the stake; another that she died from an arrow that struck her throat.

FOUR

SAINT AGATHA

D. 251

ST. AGATHA, a native of Sicily, is said to have been a person of extraordinary beauty who belonged to a noble and opulent family. These attributes attracted a man named Quintianus, the Roman governor of the district. Having made a vow of virginity at an early age, Agatha rejected his proposal of marriage, and all the attempts he made to force her to accept him. Offended by her constant refusals, Quintianus had Agatha arrested in compliance with the Emperor's edict against Christians.

When St. Agatha continued to resist, Quintianus schemed to weaken her by placing her in the care of Aphrodisia, an evil woman whose house was known for immoral activities. Because of Agatha's gentle upbringing and her firm faith, it was thought best to place her in the company of Aphrodisia's daughters, who have been described as silly, conceited girls. They had no useful occupation, but rather spent their time in idleness or foolish conversation. They were careful not to say or do anything that would shock Agatha, hoping that if she could be induced to fail in small matters such as assuming behavior comparable to theirs, she would eventually consent to larger improprieties.

The reputation of Aphrodisia was concealed from St. Agatha, who was told that in consideration of her noble birth, she was being placed in the woman's care and would remain with her until Quintianus consulted the Emperor about her future.

During the month that she stayed with Aphrodisia and her daughters, Agatha continued her usual prayers and devotions. But when she learned of the scheme to weaken her resolution to remain a virgin so that she would consent to marriage with Quintianus, St. Agatha informed Aphrodisia that she would continue to resist all their temptations and would stand firm in her innocence.

After it was realized that the plan had failed, Agatha was returned to prison—and Quintianus' anger. When next she appeared before him, she again refused his advances. This so infuriated Quintianus that he ordered her to be tortured. When this also failed, he commanded that her breasts should be cut from her body. He added that on no account should she be given food or drink, nor should a surgeon tend her, but that she should be allowed to die in the agony of her wounds. During the night, while the saint was enduring great pain and fever, St. Peter is said to have appeared in a great light to comfort her.

When the saintly virgin did not die as he expected, Quintianus had her rolled on hot coals which were mixed with broken pieces of pottery. During this torture an earthquake shook the city and produced extensive damage. The people immediately recognized this as a punishment from God for the cruelty with which the saint was being treated.

Agatha was returned to prison, and after suffering

torments because of her wounds, she offered her soul to God and expired. This took place in the year 251 in the city of Catania, Sicily. Because Agatha died on February 5, the Church observes her feast on that day.

The saint's name is mentioned in the Canon of the Mass, and she is venerated in the Churches of both the Greek and Latin Rite.

FIVE

SAINT AGNES

D. 304 OR 305

THE name Agnes, meaning "chaste" or "pure" in Greek, seems appropriate for one who is regarded among the foremost of the virgin martyrs of the primitive Church. Not only is she one of the most popular Christian saints, but her name is also commemorated in the Canon of the Mass.

Born in the City of Rome, the young saint had a brief life. St. Ambrose (d. 397) claims that Agnes was twelve years old at the time of her death, while St. Augustine (d. 430) states that she was thirteen.

Pope Damasus (d. 384) informs us that immediately after the promulgation of the Imperial Edict against the Christians, Agnes voluntarily declared herself a follower of Christ. Another source maintains that her riches and beauty excited the young noblemen of the first families of Rome, who became rivals for her hand in marriage.

When Agnes refused all of them because of her vow of chastity, one of the young men spitefully reported to the Governor that Agnes was a Christian. When a judge could not persuade her to marry nor to renounce her faith, he threatened her with confinement in a house of immorality and death by fire. Agnes calmly listened to his threats and quietly proclaimed her confidence that God would protect her body from defilement. Her only concern was the defense of her modesty, since she was later disrobed before the gaze of a heathen audience. Her flowing hair is said to have sufficiently concealed her nakedness.

St. Ambrose reported in the sixth century what took place when Agnes entered the house of sin:

> When her hair was loosed, God gave such length and thickness to her flowing tresses that they seemed to cover her completely; and when she entered the cell she found an angel of the Lord there waiting for her, who surrounded her with a dazzling light, by reason of the glory of which none might touch or look upon her. The whole room shone like the dazzling sun of midday. As Agnes knelt in prayer, Our Lord appeared and gave her a snow-white robe. The Prefect Symphonianus' son, the prime mover in the prosecution, came with some young companions to offer insult to the maiden; but suddenly falling on his face he was struck dead, and his terrified companions fled, half-dead with pain and terror. At Agnes' prayer the youth was restored to life and converted to Christianity. The people cried out that she was a sorceress and had raised him by magic.
>
> The Prefect was disposed to release her, but feared the people and the Emperor; so he went away and resigned his office to the Deputy-Prefect, Aspasius by name, who confined Agnes to prison.

The prison in which the saint was kept can be visited in the crypt of the Roman church, Sant' Agnese in Agone, located across from the Piazza Navona. In the vaulted chamber of the crypt are frescoes which depict the angels who accompanied and watched over St. Agnes.

St. Ambrose continues:

The Deputy-Prefect, Aspasius, commanded a great fire to be lighted [in the Piazza Navona] before all the people and caused Agnes to be cast into it. Immediately, the flames divided into two, scorching the people on both sides, but leaving the Saint untouched. The people ascribed this marvel to witchcraft, and the air was loud with screams and cries of "Away with the witch!" Then Aspasius, impatient at the excitement of the people, bade the executioner plunge a sword into her throat. When Agnes heard the sentence she was transported with joy and went to the place of execution more cheerfully than others go to a wedding.

St. Ambrose tells us in his sermon *De Virginibus* of the year 377 that "this child was holy beyond her years and courageous beyond human nature. . . . She stood, prayed, and then bent her neck for the stroke."

The saint died in Rome in the year 304 or 305. Burial was in the cemetery, afterwards called by her name, beside the *Via Nomentana.* After the death of Agnes, those who prayed at her grave were constantly harassed and wounded by non-Christians.

Among those who visited the grave was the saint's foster sister, St. Emerentiana, who was still a catechumen and had not yet been baptized. She was, however, baptized—not in water, but in her own blood—when she was stoned to death because of her faith. Her body was laid close to that of St. Agnes, who had died two days earlier.

Over this grave Constantia, the daughter of the Emperor Constantine, erected a basilica, *Sant' Agnes Fuori Le Mura* (St. Agnes Beyond the Walls). Below the main altar of this basilica is found a silver shrine given by Pope Paul V (1605-1621) which contains the relics of St. Agnes and those of her foster sister, St. Emerentiana.

Since the fourth century the saint's feast day has been observed on January 21. On this day each year two white lambs are offered in her basilica during High Mass and are cared for until the time for shearing. Their wool is woven into the pallia given to archbishops throughout the Church as symbolic of the jurisdiction that ultimately derives from the Holy See. A pallium, a band measuring two inches wide and decorated with six purple crosses, is placed over the archbishop's head and worn about his shoulders, falling in the front and back in the shape of a letter Y. The archbishop may wear the pallium only on special occasions, and it is always buried with him. The investiture of the pope with the pallium at his coronation is the most solemn part of the ceremony and is a symbol older than the wearing of the papal tiara.

Although some claim that the saint was killed by a sword thrust into her throat, others maintain that she was beheaded. Supporting this latter claim is the fact that the *Sancta Sanctorum* at the Lateran is in possession of the head of the saint, which was discovered in 1901 when Pope Leo XIII gave permission for the examination of the treasury after it had been closed for a number of years. According to Dr. Lapponi, an archaeologist, the dentition (arrangement of the teeth) of the skull shows conclusively that the skull belonged to a child of about thirteen years. As the result of other studies, the relic was declared to be authentic. It was further observed that the body was found without a head when the relics of the saint were examined in her church in 1605.

St. Agnes is commonly represented in art with a lamb

and a palm, the lamb being originally suggested by the resemblance of the word *agnus* (lamb) to the name Agnes.

SIX

SAINT ALBAN

D. 209

REGARDED as the first Christian martyr of Great Britain, Alban was a prominent citizen of Roman Verulamium, a place now known as St. Albans, in Hertfordshire. Although St. Alban was a pagan, he offered hospitality to a priest who was fleeing from the persecutors. The Venerable Bede (673-735) reports in his *Ecclesiastical History of the English Nation* that

> This man [the priest] Alban observed to be engaged in continual prayer and watching day and night; when on a sudden the Divine grace shining on him, Alban began to imitate the example of faith and piety which was set before him, and being gradually instructed by his wholesome admonitions, Alban cast off the darkness of idolatry and became a Christian in all sincerity of heart.

The priest remained several days with Alban before his whereabouts were discovered and reported to the authorities. Soldiers were sent to apprehend him, but

> when they came to the martyr's house, St. Alban immediately presented himself to the soldiers, instead of his guest and master, in the habit or long coat which the priest wore, and was led bound before the judge. It happened that the judge, at the time when Alban was carried before him, was

23

standing at the altar and offering sacrifice to devils. When he saw Alban, being much enraged that he should thus, of his own accord, put himself into the hands of the soldiers and incur such danger in behalf of his guest, he commanded Alban to be dragged up to the images of the devils.

St. Alban was told that since he had chosen to conceal a "rebellious and sacrilegious person" rather than deliver him up to the soldiers, he was to undergo all the punishment that the priest would have endured. Alban professed his willingness to suffer for the priest and made a noble declaration of his Christian faith. In an attempt to win him over, the judge ordered Alban to offer sacrifice to the devils—but Alban replied that all who offer sacrifice to the images would receive the everlasting pains of hell. The judge was angered at the words and ordered that Alban be scourged. However, when the tortures did not change Alban's firmness in the Faith, the judge ordered his death.

As St. Alban was being escorted to the place of execution, he came to a river which ran between the wall of the town and the arena where he was to be beheaded. Since St. Alban and his guards could not cross the bridge because of the people who had assembled there to accompany the saint, Alban remained on the shore of the river and prayed. Immediately the water "dried up, and he perceived that the water had departed and made way for him to pass." On seeing this miracle the executioner threw down his sword, fell at St. Alban's feet, and moved by divine inspiration, he asked to suffer with the saint. Both the soldier and St. Alban were martyred on the twenty-second day of June in the year 209.

Venerable Bede reports that afterwards, "A church of

wonderful workmanship, and suitable to his martyrdom, was erected, in which place there ceased not to this day the cure of sick persons and the frequent working of wonders." After the Norman Conquest in 1066, a great new church was started using bricks which the Romans had used in other buildings. Still later a monastery was built, and finally a city under the name of St. Albans, which is located approximately twenty miles north of London.

SEVEN

SAINT ANNE LYNE

1569–1601

I T IS the opinion of some, that had it not been for the close
association that existed in Elizabethan England between
the persecuted lay people and their hunted priests, the Catholic
Church in England might have disappeared altogether. The
government of the time realized this, and imposed the death
penalty, not only on priests who were discovered, but also on
every person convicted of willingly aiding, housing or maintaining them. The priests were undoubtedly heroic in remaining in England to perform their ministry, but also heroic were
those people who secretly opened their homes to gatherings
of Catholics for the celebration of Mass and the administra-
tion of the sacraments. Many Catholic housewives opened
their doors for these secret meetings, including St. Margaret
Clitherow and St. Anne Lyne (also spelled Line).

Born in the town of Dunmow in the county of Essex a little before 1570, Anne Heigham was the daughter of wealthy
Calvinist parents. When Anne and her brother reached their
teens, they announced their intention of becoming Catholics,
in direct opposition to the wishes of their parents. As a result,
both were disinherited, disowned, and were made to leave
the house.

Even though she was denied a dowry, Anne was happily married to a fervent Catholic, Roger Lyne. He, too, had lost a considerable fortune, but for a different reason—that of refusing to obey the authorities by not giving the slightest appearance of conforming to the Protestant church. Roger once said: "If I must desert either the world or God, I will desert the world, for it is good to cling to God." Shortly after his marriage, Roger was apprehended for attending Mass. Eventually released, he was permitted to go into exile in Flanders, where he died in 1594.

Anne did not follow her husband into exile, but continued the dangerous activity of harboring priests and permitting services to be secretly conducted in her home. Eventually Fr. John Gerard established a house of refuge in London for priests and other hunted Catholics. When he was thinking of finding someone to run the guest house, Anne came immediately to his mind: "I could think of no better person than Anne to take charge of it. She managed the finances, did the housekeeping, looked after the guests and dealt with strangers."

Fr. Gerard was arrested away from the guest house and was imprisoned in the Tower, but he made his escape at a time when the authorities were beginning to suspect Anne's unlawful activities. She quickly moved elsewhere and made her house a rallying point for neighboring Catholics.

On the feast of Candlemas, 1601, as Holy Mass was about to be celebrated in Anne's apartments by Fr. Francis Page, S.J., priest-catchers approached her house for an inspection. Immediately the priest unvested and mingled with the others; but when the authorities broke into the house, the altar prepared for the ceremony was all the evidence needed for Anne's arrest. She was indicted for harboring priests and was tried at the Old Bailey on February 26, 1601. Having been convicted of the charge, she was brought the next day to the gallows at Tyburn in London.

In the manuscript of the Duke of Rutland we read:

> The said Mrs. Lyne, carried next day to her execution . . . being further urged among other things by the minister that she had been a common receiver of many priests, she answered, "Where I have received one, I would to God that I had been able to receive a thousand." She behaved herself most meekly, patiently and virtuously to her last breath.

After kissing the gallows, reciting a few private prayers and blessing herself with the Sign of the Cross, she was hanged.

Two priests were executed along with St. Anne: Fr. Mark Barkworth, O.S.B. and her confessor, Fr. Roger Filcock, S.J.

Anne Lyne was canonized by Pope Paul VI in 1970 as one of the Forty Martyrs of England and Wales.

EIGHT

BLESSED ANTHONY PRIMALDI

D. 1480

THE city of Otranto in southern Italy was overrun in the year 1480 by the Turks, who rounded up a large group of the city's inhabitants and defenders and ruthlessly killed them. Archbishop Stephen Pendinelli was selected for a more cruel and painful death, being sawed into pieces by his heathen captors. When the Turks decided to torment the rest of the population they sacked homes, carried off the women and led approximately eight hundred men into a valley near the town. There the Turks offered the men the restoration of their liberty, their wives and their goods if they would renounce the Christian faith and become Moslems.

The leader of the men was Anthony Primaldi, a shoemaker who was well-known in the city as an honest workman, an honorable citizen and a good Christian. Acting as spokesman, Anthony replied that they believed that Jesus Christ was the true Son of God and that they refused to renounce their faith in Him. The Turkish general threatened them with torture and promised them a painful death if they did not renounce Jesus and acknowledge the Moslem faith.

Some of the men began to weaken under the threats,

considering, too, that the fate of their families might depend on how they would choose. But Anthony loudly addressed them: "We have fought for our city and for our lives. Now we must fight for our souls and for Jesus Christ. He died for us; we must die for Him." Anthony's appeal strengthened the men, who were then ordered to be beheaded.

After witnessing the bravery of Bl. Anthony, who was the first to die, all the other men likewise met their death while professing their faith. Their bodies were left unburied in the valley for twelve months while the Turks occupied the country, but when Otranto was retaken by Alfonso, Duke of Calabria, the Apostolic Nuncio, Bl. Angelo Carletti, ordered that some of the relics be transported to the cathedral.

In 1539 evidence was gathered from those who had escaped the massacre. One account of the Otranto martyrdoms reads:

> The witness replied that he was taken prisoner by one of the Turks and was led to a place outside the city called San Joanne de la Minerva, where about seventy men had been taken, bound, for execution. This was to frighten the witness, who was then only a boy; and one of the captain's servants said to him, "Be glad that you are not a man yet, for our lord would do the same to you." And the witness saw these men put to the sword on the spot, and killed with great cruelty . . . and there was one among them, their leader, Master Primaldi, a shoemaker, who exhorted and encouraged them all by his words, to accept their suffering and death for the love of our Lord Jesus Christ.

The veneration paid to the martyrs, and Bl. Anthony Primaldi in particular, was approved by Pope Clement XIV in 1771.

NINE

BLESSED ANTONIA MESINA

1919–1935

NESTLED in the mountainous interior of Sardinia is the little city of Orgosolo, which became the birthplace of Antonia Mesina on June 21, 1919. Her father, Agostino Mesina, who is described as being handsome, tall and lean, was a corporal in the cavalry whose assignment was to guard the rural areas around the community of Orgosolo. Antonia's mother, Grazia Raubanu, was noted for her great piety and her appreciation of her daughter Antonia, whom she frequently called "the flower of my life." There were ten children in the family, Antonia being the second-born.

Around the time of her birth, a disease known familiarly as the Spanish Fever was claiming the lives of many children. It became the practice during the epidemic for children to be confirmed at an early age. For this reason Antonia was confirmed shortly after her baptism.

During her infancy and early childhood, Antonia was like all children, being lively and playful, as well as obedient and affectionate. When she was old enough to attend school she was described as being well-liked by both her teachers and the students. Her instructors also stated that Antonia was well-behaved, precise and studious. In addition to being punctual for class, she loved the duties she was asked to perform, and she exhibited a commendable spirit of sacrifice in bending to the wishes and welfare of her classmates.

Antonia received her First Communion at the age of seven, and at the age of ten she joined an organization for young people known as the Catholic Action. She was proud to be a member and encouraged many to join the group, saying that to belong was a beautiful experience and that it "helps one to be good."

It was during Antonia's school years that her mother developed a heart condition. Unable to strain herself or lift anything heavy, Grazia found it necessary to depend almost entirely upon the help of the young Antonia, who was forced to leave school after attending elementary classes for only four years.

Taking over much of the household chores, Antonia helped her mother with the cooking, the care of the children, the cleaning and marketing. The washing of clothes and the carrying of water into the house also fell to her charge; these and her other responsibilities she performed willingly and diligently, as though she were much older. It was also noted that she was always ready to renounce her personal pleasures in favor of the needs of the family.

According to the testimony of family members and those who knew her, Antonia performed all her chores joyfully, and serenely accepted the family's modest economic condition and the hard work and sacrifice this entailed. She was also affectionate and tender with the other children in the family, and she was submissive and obedient to her parents. Her mother was proud to claim that Antonia "never once went against me."

One of Antonia's tasks was the weekly baking of bread. It was her custom to grind the grain, sift it, prepare the dough and gather wood for the baking.

On May 17, 1935, when Antonia was sixteen years old, she asked her friend Annedda Castangia to accompany her into the forest while she gathered wood for the oven. While the two girls were strolling along the path toward the woods, Antonia asked Annedda if she would like to become a member of the Catholic Action. When Annedda said that she could not join because of the cost, Antonia encouraged her to join the group by saying that there were no expenses and that there were many spiritual benefits to be gained from the good works they performed and the catechetical instruction they received.

In a deposition, Annedda reported that she could remember details of what next happened as though she had just witnessed them. After gathering a sufficient amount of wood, the girls were preparing to return home when they noticed a teenaged boy along the path. Annedda recognized him as a student from her school, but since he turned onto a different path, the girls thought no more of him. In a few moments Annedda heard Antonia scream desperately for help. The youth had sneaked up behind Antonia, grabbed her by the shoulders and was attempting to force her to the ground. Annedda tells that Antonia broke away twice, but she was caught a third time and knocked down. The would-be rapist then grabbed a rock and struck Antonia repeatedly on the face and head. Mortally wounded, Antonia continued to resist.

Annedda screamed for help and ran to the nearest house

to report what was taking place. The captain of the police was hastily summoned and he, together with other citizens, quickly rode into the woods on horseback. There they found the bloody and brutally wounded body of the sixteen-year-old Antonia. Her face was horribly disfigured from the fierce beating and was hardly recognizable as the formerly beautiful face of the virtuous little housekeeper they had always admired. After an autopsy, it was determined that Antonia's body had not been sinfully violated. Like Maria Goretti, Antonia had died a martyr of holy purity.

Antonia's companion identified the assassin; he was captured, tried and condemned to death.

During the process for her beatification, Antonia's remains were exhumed from the local cemetery. A grand procession of the townspeople, led by the bishop and several priests, accompanied the relics to the Church of the Holy Savior, where they now recline in a black marble tomb. Both the tomb and the memorial stone that marks the place of martyrdom are frequently visited by Antonia's devotees.

Antonia Mesina was beatified on Sunday, October 4, 1987 by Pope John Paul II. Also beatified during the same ceremony were Blessed Marcel Callo and Blessed Pierina Morosini—all three being twentieth-century laymen and martyrs.

TEN

SAINT AURELIUS AND SAINT NATALIA

D. 852

D URING the eighth century, when Spain first came under Mohammedan domination, the Christians were treated with tolerance, provided they did not abuse the Law of Mohammed or attempt to make converts from Islam. But during the ninth century, when the independent emirate at Cordova was established and the Emirs Abd-er-Rahman II and Mohammed I came into power, a vigorous persecution was directed toward all Spanish Catholics. One of the first to suffer was Aurelius, the son of a Moor and a Spanish woman who were both people of distinction. When both parents died during the childhood of Aurelius, he was placed in the care of his mother's sister, who educated him in the Catholic faith.

When Aurelius reached maturity, there was some cowardice in his personality, since he conformed outwardly to Islam as far as his conscience would allow—but practiced the True Religion in secret. Despite this weakness, he is credited with converting his half-Moorish wife to the Faith. Known as Sabigotho, she received the name of Natalia at her baptism.

The turning point in Aurelius' life occurred one day when

he saw a Christian merchant named John being publicly ridiculed and scourged in the public square. John was afterward dragged through the city for having spoken of the falseness of the Mohammedan religion. Feeling compunction for his cowardice in hiding his own faith, Aurelius vowed to make a public confession of his beliefs.

However, he was concerned about what would happen to his wife and two children. In discussing the matter with his wife, he learned that she, too, wanted to make a confession of her faith. Together the two Catholics consulted the imprisoned St. Eulogius, archbishop of Toledo (who was to face martyrdom in 859). St. Eulogius advised them that their profession of faith would probably result in their martyrdom, and that, as a precaution, they should make provisions for their children's material and spiritual welfare by entrusting the two girls to Christian people.

Through the grace of God, St. Aurelius thoroughly overcame his former cowardice. He and his wife began fearlessly to practice their faith and live a life of prayer and mortification. Aurelius even opened his home to fellow Christians, who joined the couple in pious practices and attendance at Holy Mass.

It was during one of these services that Aurelius, Natalia and their companions were arrested. Charged by the magistrate with being apostates from Islam, Aurelius, with his wife and companions, went heroically to the place of execution, where they were all beheaded. Their martyrdom took place on July 27, 852.

St. Eulogius, the archbishop who advised Aurelius and Natalia, had ministered to other Christians in prison, fortifying many who were condemned. He also wrote accounts of their lives, sufferings and deaths, thus leaving stories of many saints, including Sts. Aurelius and Natalia.

ELEVEN

SAINT BIBIANA

D. 363

THE Church of Santa Bibiana in Rome stands on the site where once stood the home of the noble family of Flavian, a prefect of Rome, his wife Dafrosa, and his two daughters, Demetria and Bibiana (Viviana). All four suffered for the Faith in the year 363, during the persecution of Julian the Apostate. Flavian, a zealous Christian, was eventually apprehended. For refusing to renounce his faith, he was deposed from office and branded on the face. He was then banished to Aquapendente (as *The Roman Martyrology* states) and died a few days later. Dafrosa, being equally faithful to Christ, was confined to her home. Later she was carried outside the gates of the city and beheaded. Bibiana and her sister, Demetria, were deprived of all that they owned, suffering extreme poverty for five months—a time that was made meritorious by their prayers and fasting.

Brought before Governor Apronianus, Demetria made a generous confession of her faith. A biographer states that after this declaration she dropped dead before him. Apronianus then gave orders that Bibiana should be placed in the care of a wicked woman named Rufina, who was extremely successful in persuading young girls to indulge in sinful occupations. But when all Rufina's efforts failed, Apronianus became enraged at the courage and perseverance of the young girl and passed the sentence of death upon her. She was to be tied to a pillar and whipped with scourges loaded with lead. Bibiana died during this beating. Her body was left exposed in the open air so that scavenging dogs might feed on it, but after two days the untouched body was carried away by a priest named John and was buried at Bibiana's home beside the remains of her mother and sister.

In the year 465 a pious lady named Olympia built a church over the tomb. This church was consecrated by Pope Simplicius and was later repaired by Honorius III. When it was again repaired in 1628 by Bernini for Urban VIII, the relics of Bibiana, Demetria and Dafrosa were placed in an oriental alabaster shrine under the high altar.

Inside the Church of St. Bibiana is a statue of the saint by Bernini, and at the back of the church, protected by an iron grille, is the column of red porphyry to which she was tied when she was scourged.

TWELVE

SAINT BLANDINA

D. 177

F RANCE may seem too distant from persecuted Rome to
have produced second-century martyrs, but in those
times Lyons and Vienne (located in what was then known as
Gaul) had an organized community of Christians which has
given us forty-eight heroes and heroines of the Faith. These
are all known, but prominent among them is St. Blandina,
a slave, who was a victim of the persecution under Marcus
Aurelius. What we know of these martyrs is given to us in a
letter which is preserved by Eusebius of Caesarea in Book V
of his *Ecclesiastical History*. In this letter, which was addressed
to the churches of Asia and Phrygia, the social ostracism and
physical torments of these martyrs are carefully outlined.

The letter, which is described as one of the most precious
documents of Christian antiquity, recounts that orders had
been given for general arrests, and this included some of the
servants who were not Christians. Afraid of being tortured,
some of these captives falsely accused the Christians "of feed-
ing on human flesh like Thyestes and of committing incest
like Oedipus, as well as other abominations which it is unlawful for us even to think of, and which we can scarcely believe
ever to have been perpetrated by men."

Although the charges were untrue, shame and torment afflicted the pious souls on hearing themselves charged with such disgraceful acts. Eusebius gives us some idea of the resulting public attitude toward the Christians:

> When these things were made public, all men were exasperated against us, including some who had formerly shown friendliness towards us. . . . The fury of the mob, the governor and the soldiers fell most heavily upon Sanctus, a deacon from Vienne, on Maturus, newly baptized but a noble combatant, on Attalus, a native of Pergamos, who had always been a pillar and support of the Church, and on Blandina, a slave.

At first the martyrs suffered general indignities including insults, stone throwing, blows and plundering—but gradually the non-Christians grew so furious at the crimes alleged against the Christians that more serious punishments were demanded. The Christians were then subjected to torture and were put to death in various ways.

St. Blandina was of such a delicate constitution that her mistress, who was also a victim of the persecution, "was in distress lest she [St. Blandina] should not be able, through the weakness of her body, to be bold enough even to make confession [of her faith]." But fortified with the grace of God, St. Blandina displayed so much courage and withstood so much abuse while imprisoned that Eusebius relates,

> They took turns in torturing her in every way from morning until evening, and they themselves confessed that they had nothing left to do to her and they marveled that she still remained alive, seeing that her whole body was broken and open, and they testified that any one of these tortures was sufficient to destroy life, even when they had not been magnified and multiplied.

Always mindful of the false charges leveled against the Christians, St. Blandina, in spite of her tortured body, repeatedly affirmed, "I am a Christian woman and nothing wicked happens among us."

With three of her companions, St. Blandina was brought into the amphitheater to be subjected to wild beasts. St. Blandina, however, was the only one hung from a stake. Remaining there with her arms extended, she served as a symbol of the Crucifixion, giving courage to her friends. When none of the beasts would touch her, she was removed from the stake and taken back to the jail. Eusebius records that

> In addition to all this, on the last day of the gladiatorial sports Blandina was again brought in [to the amphitheater] with Ponticus, a boy of about 15 years, and they had been brought in every day to see the torture of the others, and efforts were made to force them to swear by the idols, and the mob was furious against them so that there was neither pity for the youth of the boy nor respect for the sex of the woman.

Ponticus, encouraged by the example of St. Blandina, endured many tortures before dying heroically. As for the blessed Blandina:

> After scourging, after the beasts, after the gridiron, she was at last put in a net and thrown to a bull. She was tossed about a long time by the beast, having no more feeling for what happened to her through her hope and hold on what had been trusted to her and her converse with Christ. And so she, too, was sacrificed and the heathens themselves confessed that never before among them had a woman suffered so much and so long.

The remains of the martyrs were not given the Christian

burial they deserved, but were left exposed for six days. After being subjected to many indignities and outrageous acts, the bodies were at last burned and the ashes thrown into the Rhone River. The year of St. Blandina's death was 177.

THIRTEEN

SAINT BONIFACE
OF TARSUS

D. 306

BONIFACE is described as having been "a big fine figure of a man, with a heavy shock of hair." Prior to his conversion, he was also described as having been fond of wine and "debauchery." By way of making less of these vices, one biographer promptly adds that he was extremely generous to the poor.

When Boniface became acquainted with a formerly dissolute Roman lady named Aglae, who had become converted, he was so impressed that he followed her example and was baptized.

By way of pleasing Aglae and doing penance for his past sins, Boniface journeyed from Rome to the East in search of certain relics. Upon reaching Tarsus, he saw a group of confessors being led to torture. He kissed their chains and attempted to defend them. For this he was condemned to death, and was subsequently beheaded.

Aglae eventually obtained the relics of Boniface. These she placed in an oratory fifty stadia from Rome. It is thought that this church was built by Algae specifically to enshrine the relics of Boniface. The church was rebuilt by Pope Honorius III, and in 1216 the bodies of St. Alexius and St. Boniface were discovered and placed under the high altar. These relics were last seen and identified in 1603. In this church are also kept the relics of Aglae. The church was first named for St. Alexius, but later was given a double patronage and is known as the Church of St. Alexius (Sant' Alessio) and St. Boniface.

FOURTEEN

SAINT CASSIAN

D. 304

S T. CASSIAN was a schoolmaster in the city of Imola, some twenty-five miles west of Ravenna, Italy. As a Catholic he conscientiously taught young boys to read and write and gave them a fine example by the Christian virtues which he practiced in the performance of his duties.

When a persecution against the Church reached Imola about the year 304, Cassian was interrogated by the Governor of the province. Since he steadfastly affirmed his allegiance to the Christian faith and repeatedly declined to sacrifice to the gods, the prefect condemned him to death and ordered that he should suffer in the place of his employment.

At that time it was the custom in schools to write upon wax that had been smoothed on a board of boxwood. The letters were formed in the wax with an iron stylus, or pen, which was sharp at one end for marking, but blunt at the other end for correcting and smoothing.

When the judgment was rendered, Cassian was brought to his classroom and was disrobed before two hundred boys. It was then ordered that his death should be accomplished at the hands of his students, who were told to stab their teacher with their iron pens. Whether out of vengeance for past corrections, or whether they were forced to do so, it is said that the boys threw their tablets, pens and knives at the saint's face and head and often broke them upon his body. Others cut his flesh or stabbed him with their pens, while others made sport of cutting letters out of his skin. Covered with blood and wounded in every part of his body, the saint withstood the torment in a heroic fashion until death released him from his agony.

St. Cassian was buried by the Christians at Imola, where his relics were honored with a splendid shrine.

Prudentius, who poetically recorded the manner of the saint's death in *Peristephanon* IX, tells that while on his way to Rome he visited and prayed before the martyr's tomb. He also mentions a picture over the altar depicting the martyrdom of the saint.

FIFTEEN

SAINT CECILIA

D. 177

CECILIA was a member of a distinguished Roman family. She outwardly complied with all that pertained to the customs and manner of dress that were expected of a young woman of her position, but, unknown to others, she fasted often and wore a coarse garment beneath her clothes.

Despite her desire to remain a virgin, she was given in marriage to Valerianus, a nobleman. The young saint obediently participated in the marriage ceremony, but when she was alone with her bridegroom, Cecilia was successful in persuading him to respect her vow of virginity and converted him to the Faith. Following his baptism, Valerianus was favored with a vision of Cecilia's guardian angel that greatly comforted him during his future trials.

Valerianus and his brother Tiburtius, who was also converted by Cecilia, were later martyred for the Faith. Then Cecilia was arrested for having buried their bodies; she was given the choice of sacrificing to heathen gods or being put to death. Cecilia chose to die for the Faith, as had Valerianus and Tiburtius.

Because Cecilia was a member of a distinguished and well-known family, Turcius Almachius, the prefect of Rome, thought it best to execute her in private instead of in public, which might bring criticism from various quarters. For this reason it was decided that she should be placed in the bath (the *caldarium*) of her home, which was to be kept intensely heated until the suffocating atmosphere deprived her of life.

Cecilia entered the place of martyrdom and remained there the rest of the day and night without being harmed. Since this method of execution was not successful, she was ordered to be beheaded in the same place. Due to inexperience or lack of courage, the executioner failed to sever her head with the three blows prescribed by law. Cecilia lay dying on the pavement of her bath, fully conscious, with her head half severed, until she expired three days later. The position of her fingers, three extended on her right hand and one on the left, was accepted as her final profession of faith in the Holy Trinity.

Christians clothed Cecilia's body in rich robes of silk and gold and placed it in a cypress coffin in the same position in which she had died. She was first interred in the Catacomb of St. Callistus. In 822 Pope Pascal I had the body removed, with the relics of Valerianus and Tiburtius, to the Basilica of St. Cecilia.

An exhumation of the incorrupt body was made in 1599. A sculpture made by Stefano Maderno at this time represents the saint in the exact posture of her body. The statue is now situated slightly below and in front of the high altar. The marble slab on this altar is the one on which the saint was placed during the attempted suffocation, and it may be the one on which she died. The body of the saint, together with the relics of Valerianus and Tiburtius, are interred in the crypt of the church.

Cecilia is often depicted in art with an organ to express what was often attributed to her in panegyrics and poems based on her *Acts,* that "while the musicians played at her nuptials, she sang in her heart to God only." When the Academy of Music was founded in Rome in 1584, Cecilia was made its patroness, whereupon her veneration as patroness of church music became universal.

SIXTEEN

BLESSED CHARLES
THE GOOD

1083–1127

CHARLES was called "The Good" by his subjects because of his virtues and his wise and kindly rule as the Count of Flanders and Amiens. His father, St. Canute, King of Denmark, had been slain in St. Alban's Church in 1086.

Born about the year 1083, Charles was only three years old at the time of his father's death. Following this tragedy, his mother, Adela van Vlaanderen, took Charles to the court of her father, Robert de Frison (Fries), count of Flanders. Charles' grandfather and an uncle, Robert II, greatly influenced him and trained him in all chivalrous exercises. In due time, Charles earned the honor of being knighted.

When his uncle, Robert II, joined the Crusade to do battle against the infidels in Palestine, Charles went with him and distinguished himself in combat. Upon his return home, Charles again engaged in battle, this time against the English.

When Robert II died, he was succeeded by his son Baldwin who, having no children, designated his cousin Charles to succeed him. Baldwin was also instrumental in arranging Charles' marriage with Margaret, daughter of Renault, count of Clermont, whose dowry consisted of the County of Amiens. Charles assisted his cousin Baldwin in the government of Flanders, so that when Baldwin died, the people, having become accustomed to Charles, received him happily.

Trouble was brewing, however, in the form of other claimants, and for several years Charles had to face a great deal of resentment and resistance to his authority. His most serious opponent was Countess Clemence of Burgundy, the widow of his uncle Robert. She supported her niece's husband, William de Loo, viscount of Ypres. The Countess was successful in organizing an uprising among the Flemings of the seacoast, while the feudal nobles in her district of Fumes joined her troops, hoping to increase their power. They succeeded in taking the city of Audenarde and invaded West Flanders, but Charles' army soundly defeated them.

The reputation of Charles was such that he was offered the imperial dignity after the death of Henry V. He refused this honor, as well as an offer of the crown of Jerusalem. In humbly refusing these honors Charles expressed the intention of devoting himself entirely to the Flemish people. This, he thought, was more in keeping with the will of God.

When external problems were under control, Charles devoted himself to formulating laws, which he then strictly enforced. By his example, he brought his country to a high level of culture. Being simple and modest, he detested flattery. He observed the fasts of the Church and performed other penances. When he was criticized for defending the poor against the rich, he said, "It is because I know so well the needs of the poor and the pride of the rich." He detested blasphemy to such an extent that any member of his household who swore by God's name was punished by a fast of bread and water for forty days.

The peace and security of the country seemed threatened when there was an eclipse of the sun in August, 1124, which the irreligious accepted as a sign of forthcoming troubles. Trouble did indeed visit the land, in the form of a famine which came a year later. The grain that sprang up was destroyed by winds and storms. The poor suffered greatly and were forced to beg at the strongholds of the great lords. But even though the poor were sick from disease and malnutrition, they failed to arouse the sympathy of those who could have helped them, and many died by the wayside.

Charles did all he could to relieve the victims of the disaster. Daily at Bruges, and at each of his castles, he fed a hundred poor men, and at Ypres he distributed 7,800 two-pound loaves in one day. He reprimanded certain nobles for allowing men to die at their gates, forbade the brewing of beer in order to save grain, set a fixed price for the sale of wine, and ordered the land to be sown in grain—and in peas or beans, which grow faster. When he was informed that certain nobles were hoarding grain to sell later at a higher price, Charles and his almoner, Tancmar, forced them to sell at once and at a reasonable price. This so infuriated these nobles that the chief of the profiteers, Lambert, and his brother Bertulphus, the dean of St. Donatian at Bruges, devised a plot to murder Charles. Also conspiring in this endeavor were Erembald, the chief magistrate of Bruges, together with his five sons, who resented Charles for having corrected their violent activities.

It was the custom of the holy Count to walk barefoot each morning to the Church of St. Donatian to attend Holy Mass.

One morning, before starting on his walk, he was warned that there was a conspiracy against him. He replied, "We are always in the midst of dangers, but we belong to God. If it be His will, can we die in a better cause than that of justice and truth?" While he was reciting the Psalm *Miserere* before the altar of Our Lady in the church, the conspirators went into action. Wielding swords, his enemies cut off one of his arms; his head was slashed by Bertulphus' nephew, Borchard. Thus Bl. Charles died on March 2, 1127. He was about forty-four years old.

The relics of Bl. Charles the Good, who merited the martyr's crown, are kept in the Cathedral of Bruges (Sint-Salvatorskathedraal). Devotion to the holy martyr was approved and encouraged by Pope Leo XIII in 1882.

SEVENTEEN

SAINT CHARLES LWANGA AND COMPANIONS

(THE 22 MARTYRS OF UGANDA)

D. 1885-1887

IT TOOK considerable courage for twenty-five-year-old Fr. Simon Lourdel of the White Fathers of Africa to venture into Uganda with his one companion, Brother Amans. The country was inhabited in 1879 by natives who pillaged, massacred and exercised all manner of debauchery. They occasionally offered human victims to the spirits and took natives from other tribes into captivity. There were also sorcerers who took pleasure in terrorizing the country.

Despite the dangers, the good priest and his companion made it safely in a small boat to the village of King Mutesa of Uganda. There they were cordially received and were later joined by their three companions, who had been left some distance away at the village of Kagweye.

Fr. Lourdel lost no time in speaking of the Christian faith to the King, who seemed interested until he was told that he must keep only one wife and send all the others away. In his meetings with the King, Fr. Lourdel became aware of a dangerous enemy in the person of the King's chief assistant,

Katikiro, who seemed to resent the white-robed missionaries. Other members of the court also seemed to mistrust the priests; wild rumors were spread about them, and sinister plots were said to be planned by them.

The priests, however, were able to teach the gospel and were successful in baptizing a large number of natives. When Fr. Lourdel learned that others were planning on capturing the priests and putting them to death by fire, he and his companions prepared to leave. They gathered together the children they had ransomed and as many of the newly baptized as wanted to come with them. They set off by boat to the village of Kagweye, where they arrived on January 4, 1883.

Almost two years later, the priests learned that King Mutesa, knowing that he was about to die, had called for the young Christian, Joseph Mukasa, the chief of the royal pages and one of the first to have been baptized by Fr. Lourdel.

After the King sent away his wives, Joseph Mukasa comforted the dying leader, but it is unknown if the King was baptized—although it is known that the King died in Joseph's arms on October 10, 1884.

Succeeding his father as leader of the tribe was King Mwanga, who was only eighteen years old. He had always seemed to like "The Praying Ones" and sent word that the priests were once more welcome in Uganda. He even went so far as to send canoes to bring the missionaries and their belongings to his village.

The priests' return in July of 1885 was heartwarming. The natives were pleased to see them again, and the priests, for their part, were happy to learn that their convert, twenty-six-year-old Joseph Mukasa, and the other Christians had instructed several hundred natives, who were now awaiting Baptism.

One who was not pleased to see the return of the priests was Katikiro, who had served the old King as his chief assistant. He remained in the same position of influence to assist the youthful King Mwanga. Since the young King looked favorably toward the "Praying Ones," Katikiro devised a plan to kill his master and to install as the new leader Mwanga's brother, who was more inclined to agree with him that the priests posed a great threat and should be banished from the country. But before this could be accomplished, three Christians learned of the planned assassination and warned King Mwanga. Katikiro was successful in pleading his ignorance of the plot but, from then on, his hatred of the Christians increased.

When Katikiro learned in November of 1885 that an Anglican bishop, the Rev. Hannington, and his assistants planned on passing through Uganda to the Lake Victoria area, Katikiro persuaded the King that the priests were sending for still more white men who would all plot to dethrone him. After learning of their plot to massacre the Anglican Bishop, Fr. Lourdel pleaded for their lives and begged the King to greet the new arrivals with respect and courtesy. The priest's efforts were futile, since Hannington was massacred, together with some of his companions.

Fr. Lourdel visited the King to learn the truth of the rumor that many of the Anglicans had been killed, but he received only silence for his questions. Joseph Mukasa also spoke to the King about the matter, but this was a grave mistake, since Katikiro was successful in persuading the King that Joseph Mukasa was not only against him, but was also planning some revenge for the killing of Hannington.

The King had other reasons for distrusting Joseph, since Joseph, as chief of the pages, customarily hid the boys when the King intended to entice them into committing sins of impurity.

The next morning, when Joseph Mukasa was returning from the Mission Chapel after receiving Holy Communion, he was apprehended on the King's orders. While his wrists were being securely tied, Joseph asked, "Come now, what are you doing? If I must die for my faith, do you think that I am going to try to escape? A Christian who dies for God does not fear death!" He was brought into the woods, where a fiery death awaited him. But Mukajanga, the chief of the executioners, displaying an uncommon compassion, refused to let him die by fire. Instead, Mukajanga drew his sword. Joseph then pronounced his final words, "Tell the King that I pardon him gladly for killing me without reason, but that I advise him to repent. If not, I shall be his accuser before the judgment seat of God."

Joseph then knelt in prayer and in a moment, with one strike of the blade, he was decapitated. His body was thrown on the fire, where it was devoured by flames. It was on November 15, 1885 that Joseph Mukasa became the first native of Uganda to die for the Faith.

The executioner reported to the King what had taken place and repeated the victim's final words, which were to prove troublesome to the superstitious King. Katikiro, for his part, was once more successful in turning the King against the Christians by claiming that Joseph would be only the first of many dangerous Christians to be killed. After all, what could be expected of those who do not sacrifice to the gods of the tribe, who neither pillage, massacre, or engage in war? What would happen to the Kingdom if most or all of the King's subjects became Christians?

The priests and their congregation drew new courage from the example of Joseph Mukasa and vowed to die bravely for the Faith if the King called for their assassination. Inspired by the martyrdom, many asked for instruction and begged for Baptism; in one week, there were more than one hundred baptisms. One of those who was baptized at this time was Charles Lwanga, the strongest athlete of the court, "the most handsome man of the Kingdom of the Uganda." He had previously worked under Joseph Mukasa and was now his replacement as the chief of the royal pages.

For almost six months, from October 1885 to March 1886, there was almost complete peace in the village. The King had retired to his summer home some distance from the village and was known to throw only occasional rages against the Christians. But one day after his return, when he called for his young servant, a fourteen-year-old boy name Mwafu, the son of the dreaded Katikiro, he learned that Mwafu was nowhere to be found. When Mwafu finally appeared before the King and offered as his excuse that Denis Sebuggwawo had been teaching him catechism, the King flew into a rage.

Denis, who had been standing nearby, thinking that his friend was in danger, presented himself to the King's fury. Snatching a lance, the King brutally pierced it through Denis' throat and contemptuously left the sixteen-year-old boy where he lay on the ground. The boy died the next day, after a night spent in prayer and extreme pain. Denis Sebuggwawo thus became the second martyr of Uganda.

The King bitterly regretted the recall of the priests and became a staunch enemy of the Christians. Crazed with hatred, he gave orders that the gates of the compound should be closed and that guards should make certain no one left the village. He had a fire lit and had drums beaten all night as a signal for the assembly of executioners. The King knew that among his pages there were many Christians. These would be found out and killed as a punishment.

During the night, while the drums sounded, Charles Lwanga assembled the pages and other Christians. They prayed constantly that those who would die for the Faith would do so courageously in the name of Jesus Christ. Charles also baptized the boy pages, Mugagga, Mbaga, Gyavira and Kizito, all of whom had been longing to be received into the Church.

The next day, while the servants went about their duties, Charles Lwanga, as chief of the pages, was ordered to gather the boys before the hut of the King. When they approached the King, they prostrated themselves in the usual manner. Then the King ordered those who did not pray to stand to one side. Those who prayed should line up outside.

Charles was the first to leave. Kizito, a twelve-year-old lad who had been baptized the night before, followed him, as did the newly baptized Mbaga, Gyavira and Mugagga. Athanasius Bazzekuketta also went outside, as did Ambrose Kibuka and Achilles Kiwanuka, who were cousins. When all had assembled, the King asked if they were all Christians and if they wished to remain so, even to death. When all had professed their faith and their willingness to die for it, the death sentence was passed and the executioners moved toward them. Mukajanga, the chief executioner, who had martyred Joseph

Mukasa, also moved forward. When he did so, he noticed among the Christians and a few condemned Anglicans his own son, Mbaga Tuzinde. When Mbaga refused to recant, the executioner reluctantly accepted the inevitable.

The group then began to move slowly, but valiantly, toward the place of execution seventeen miles away, a wooded area known as Namugongo. None of the condemned uttered a cry, shed a tear or made a gesture of defense, but moved obediently under the eyes of several guards.

When the line passed the hut where James Buzabaliawo was imprisoned, the King ordered that this Christian should also join the line. James accepted his fate and humbly told the King, "In Heaven I will pray to God for you."

Standing nearby was Fr. Lourdel, who had been trying to approach the prisoners but had been prevented from doing so by the guards, who vehemently forbade the priest to even speak to them. The prisoners, however, smiled and motioned to him. Fr. Lourdel could do nothing but give them his blessing and his prayers.

Voluntarily joining the line was Bruno Serunkuma, one of the King's bodyguards who had secretly taken instructions at night. Also added to the line was Pontian Ngondwe, whom the Kabaka had at one time given the charge of growing bananas. When Pontian asked that he be martyred without delay, the guards were delighted to comply with his request. After knocking him down, one of the executioners raised his lance and ripped Pontian's body in several places before cutting off his head. Pontian was between thirty-five and forty years of age.

While the line was still on its way, another young man tightly held by two executioners was added to the group of

Christians. He was Mukasa Kiriwawanvu, a frequent visitor to the Mission. When Gyavira saw his friend he smiled broadly and moved toward him, saying, "I am glad to die with you for our Master Jesus Christ."

When the prisoners were near the Village of Mengo they were tied securely with ropes and were forced to lie on the ground. To make certain they would not move or escape, slave-yokes were placed on their necks. The slave-yoke consisted of a stick, the end of which branched into a V. When this fork was placed over the neck of the prisoner and shoved into the ground, it pressed against the throat, causing pain and preventing the prisoner from moving.

When the prisoners were being secured in this manner, two of the guards arrived with twenty-year-old Athanasius Bazzekuketta, who previously had the task of guarding the King's treasures. Athanasius had tripped and fallen along the way. As a punishment, he was severely beaten. He was then taken to a place where ashes and pieces of bone littered a small area. The guards indicated that this was the place where Joseph Mukasa had been killed some six months earlier. This was also to be the place of martyrdom for Athanasius, whose chest was swiftly pierced by a lance. Afterward the executioner jumped repeatedly on his victim before the martyr's head, arms and legs were cut off and the body hacked to pieces.

The next morning, May 27, when the yokes on the prisoners were removed, Gonzaga Gonza stood up with great difficulty. The day before, with his shackles cutting into his flesh, Gonzaga had bled profusely during a five-mile walk. Because weakness and pain now made it impossible to walk, he fell to the ground. When one of the executioners saw that Gonzaga was unable to continue on the journey, he decided to finish him off where he lay and killed him with a thrust of a lance. Gonzaga died without making a sound.

Bruno Serunkuma, who had willingly surrendered, was suffering severely from the tight ropes, the ravages of a high fever and an unquenchable thirst. When the line of prisoners passed the hut of his brother, he called for his brother to bring him a little banana wine. But Bruno must have remembered the thirst of Our Lord on the Cross, because he refused the drink offered him and continued on.

Meanwhile another Christian arrived; it was Luke Banabakintu, who had taught catechism to the young pages. He had been stopped at the same time as Matthias Mulumba, a forty-five-year-old Christian man who was the father of a family. Both were condemned to die with the pages, but Matthias stopped along the way and asked to be martyred where he stood, at a place known as Kampala. The executioner complied. Following the orders of Katikiro, Matthias was tortured with unbelievable cruelty.

While the flesh was being cut from his body, Matthias moaned and prayed, "*Katonda! Katonda!* (My God! My God!)." After sawing off his hands and feet, the executioner had the cruelty to tie up the severed arteries and veins in order to stop the bleeding and thus prolong his agony. Matthias was left to die, but two days later, when natives were cutting reeds nearby, they heard a voice moaning, "Water. Water." When they discovered the butchered and bleeding body, they ran away, terrified. Several days later they found that the body had been dried by the sun.

During this time, Katikiro sent armed men to find the

Christian relatives of Matthias. They found and questioned the thirty-five-year-old Noah Mawaggali, a maker of pipes and earthen pottery. When Noah acknowledged that he was a Christian and would not stop praying as they had asked him to, he was seized, stabbed and tied to a tree, with his arms extended to each side. Before he died, he endured the additional torture of having his flesh torn away, piece by piece.

His younger sister boldly surrendered, asking to be killed with the others, but she was only imprisoned. Manaku, who had changed her name to Matilda at her Baptism, became the first girl in Uganda to embrace virginity for the love of Jesus Christ.

Since the prisoners were to die by fire, a great many trees and branches had to be gathered into a large pyre. During the six days that the pyre was being prepared, the prisoners suffered from their shackles and slave-yokes. They did not spend the time idly, however, but in constant prayer and in exhorting one another to courage and trust in God.

On June 2, when the enormous pyre was ready, war drums were brought out and savage chants were sung throughout the night. The following morning, the group was marched to the pyre by the guards, who had painted themselves in a frightening manner with red clay.

Suddenly from the forest ran the young boy, Mbaga, the son of the chief executioner, Mukajanga. He had previously been removed from the group by his father, who had hoped to save his life. But the boy had escaped, and he ran happily to join his comrades.

On the way to the pyre, the condemned were tapped on the head with a long reed held by a chief executioner named

Senkole. This tap on the head was a pagan rite to prevent the souls of those killed from returning to harass the King. If a tap was not given, the prisoner was reprieved. For reasons not known, three of the prisoners were spared. These were Denis Kamyuka, Simeon Sebuta and Charles Werabe. To them we owe the details of what is known of the martyrdom of the Christians of Uganda.

According to a traditional procedure, the chief executioners had the right to reserve for themselves one of the condemned, whom they could torture as they pleased. Chosen for this special treatment was Charles Lwanga, who signaled to his comrades, "I shall see you very soon! Very shortly I shall join you in heaven!" Charles was made to wait while the prisoners were placed on reed mats that had been prepared the night before. Each was then rolled on his mat until he was enclosed in a bundle of wood which was securely tied about him.

The three who had been spared then saw the distraught Mukajanga release his son from the bundle of wood and plead with the boy to renounce his faith. But Mbaga only asked to die with the others. In an effort to spare his son the torture of being burned alive, Mukajanga had one of the executioners beat his son on the head with a club. The boy was killed instantly by the blow. The body was then placed in the reed fencing and was brought to the pyre.

To the amazement of the guards and the executioners, the prisoners prayed aloud. "You can very well burn my body," Bruno Serunkama said, "but you cannot burn my soul, for it belongs to God." The pyre was then lit. After the fire consumed its victims, the attention of the executioners turned to Charles Lwanga.

When Charles saw that a special pyre was being prepared for him, he asked to be untied so that he could help in arranging the place of torture. In a peaceful and almost cheerful manner, Charles arranged the wood and sticks and then laid down upon them. When the executioner announced that Charles would be burned over a slow fire, Charles answered that he was very glad to be dying for the True Faith.

The fire was ignited. With the flames licking at his feet, Charles stiffened, but did not utter a single cry. The torture lasted a long time. Charles twisted under the pain, but remained ever faithful to his religion and was heard to moan repeatedly, "*Katonda*! (O my God!)."

On the way back to the village, Denis Kamyuka heard one of the executioners pronounce words to which the others agreed, "We have killed many men in our time, but never such as these! The others did nothing but moan and weep, but these prayed right to the end!"

A few days later, two Christians from a nearby village came secretly to the places of torture, collected a few charred bones and ashes and brought them to the Mission Chapel. These relics were deposited in a reliquary, where they are still kept, in the Church of St. Mary of Rubaga.

Katikiro, the hateful assistant at court and initiator of the whole drama, had remained at Namugongo, but he was far from satisfied with his vengeance and was alert for still more Christians. It was then that he remembered thirty-year-old Andrew Kaggwa, an officer in the King's army. Not only had Andrew been a friend of Joseph Mukasa, the first martyr, but he had contributed his influence to the return of the missionaries.

Fortunately for Andrew, he had received Holy Communion the night before his capture and was thus fortified to accept what was planned for him. On May 26, 1886, after he denied many false charges, his arm was cut off and given to Katikiro, who had asked for this token. Andrew was then beheaded and his body cut into pieces.

Adolph Ludigo and Anatole Kiriggwajjo also died for the Faith, but the last of the martyrs was John Mary Muzeyi. He had been a page to the old King Mutesa. As a young man he had often ransomed slaves, whom he took to the mission. He had shown admirable courage in taking care of the sick during an epidemic of the plague.

John Mary was absent on the morning when the pages were condemned to death, but Katikiro remembered him and called for his arrest, which took place on January 27, 1887, while John Mary was walking along a path. His head was quickly cut off and his body thrown into muddy water. A woman who had known John Mary witnessed the execution and later told the details of his death.

The proud leaders of the tribe who had been instrumental in the martyrdom of the Christians all experienced horrible deaths. King Mwanga was first of all dethroned by a revolution which obliged him to flee. He was then captured by the English, who led him in chains to a prison where he soon died at the age of thirty-four.

During the revolution, Katikiro was captured and killed by two of his servants. His body was left to be eaten by dogs.

Mukajanga, the executioner, was afflicted with a horrible skin disease which covered his entire body with infected sores. His chief assassin, Senkole, was snatched and devoured by a crocodile along the banks of a lake.

Built on the very spot where the royal hut of King Mwanga formerly stood is the Cathedral of Rubaga. The country of Uganda now has several dioceses, each one having its minor seminary, and there are three major seminaries for all the dioceses. The White Fathers, as well as other missionary priests and religious, continue to help in spreading the True Faith. Also assisting are many natives who became members of religious orders.

During the years following the persecution, news of the heroic deaths of the Ugandan martyrs became well-known due to the testimony of Denis Kamyuka, who had been saved from a fiery death. During an ecclesiastical inquiry, Denis repeated the details that had surrounded the death of the martyrs. Finally on June 6, 1920, Pope Benedict XV proclaimed the twenty-two martyrs Blessed. Fourteen years later, Charles Lwanga, the chief of the pages, was designated the patron of the African Youth of Catholic Action. The martyrs were canonized by Pope Paul VI on June 22, 1964.

EIGHTEEN

SAINT COSMAS AND SAINT DAMIAN

D. 303

THE Eastern Church venerates a small group of saints who are called "the moneyless ones" because they practiced their professions without accepting payment. The best-known of these saints are twin brothers Cosmas and Damian, who were born in the middle of the third century in Egea, a city in Cilicia which belonged to the Patriarchate of Antioch, in Asia Minor. They studied medicine in Syria and, as devout Christians, imitated the Divine Healer while traveling through the towns and villages of their native country. They cured countless infirmities without accepting payment and saved the souls of many by converting them to the True Faith.

In the year 303, during the persecution of the Christian Church by the Roman Emperor Diocletian, their charitable endeavors came to the attention of the authorities. They were arrested for being Christians and remained true to their faith under torture. The prefect Lisia, in his office as governor of Syria and therefore the supreme magistrate of Rome, sentenced them to death, together with their brothers: Antimo, Leonzio and Euprepio. Various legendary accounts relate that they were miraculously preserved from death by fire, drowning, stoning, etc., although the sword finally claimed them when both were beheaded. Although their martyrdom is universally considered to have taken place in September of the year 303, there is controversy concerning the place. It is generally thought that they died in either Egea in Cilicia, their native city, or Ciro (Cyrrhus, Cyr) in Syria, where they were buried. Over their tombs a basilica was constructed, which was later enlarged by Constantine.

When Felix IV (526-530) was elected pope, there were already five churches in Rome dedicated to Cosmas and Damian. Pope Felix, who was particularly devoted to them, decided to erect in their honor a basilica which would be their principal sanctuary. The Roman Temple of Romulus and an adjacent room which had been the library of the Vespasian's Forum were converted into a church and dedicated to the two physicians. In this church Pope Felix placed an altar of peacock-streaked marble, which remains in its original location, although poor drainage has reduced it to crypt-level. In this crypt, which is really a lower church, the Holy Sacrifice is celebrated each Sunday. Originally consecrated by Pope Felix, the altar was reconsecrated by Pope Gregory the Great (590-604), who placed principal relics of the two saints beneath the altar.

In the upper basilica, behind the high altar, is found the Monumental Mosaic on which construction was begun during the pontificate of Pope Felix. Sts. Cosmas and Damian are depicted holding their crowns of martyrdom. They are being led by the Apostles Peter and Paul to Christ, who is the central figure.

SAINT COSMAS AND SAINT DAMIAN

Sts. Cosmas and Damian are regarded as patrons of physicians, surgeons, druggists and dentists. The names of both Saints are mentioned in the Canon of the Mass and in the Litany of the saints. They are particularly remembered each year on September 26, when their feast day is liturgically celebrated.

NINETEEN

SAINT DYMPHNA

D. 650

DYMPHNA was the only child of a pagan king and a Christian queen who ruled a section of Ireland in the seventh century. Dymphna bore a striking resemblance to her beautiful mother, an attribute that was to threaten her purity and caused the loss of her life.

After the death of the Queen, the inconsolable King, on the verge of mental collapse, consented to the court's entreaties that he distract his thoughts from his beloved wife by marrying a second time. The King's only requirement was that the new wife should resemble his first. Since no one in the country could compare except the daughter, she was suggested as the replacement for her deceased mother. The emotional turmoil of the King allowed this sinful suggestion to seem plausible.

When the illicit marriage was proposed, Dymphna confided the news to her confessor, a pious priest named Gerebern, by whom her mother and other members of the family had been instructed in the Faith. He advised Dymphna to explain to her father the sinful and horrible nature of his proposal, and to pray to God that he would change his mind and ask God for forgiveness for ever having considered such a union.

Dymphna obeyed her confessor, but the King was deaf to all her arguments. He appointed a certain day on which the ceremony should take place. Knowing too well the obstinate and vindictive nature of the pagan King, and realizing that it was useless to attempt to change his plans, Gerebern decided that flight was the only means of preserving Dymphna's purity.

Secret plans were made for Gerebern, as well as the court jester and his wife, to accompany Dymphna in her escape from the country. After crossing the sea to the coast of Belgium, they traveled inland and settled twenty-five miles from Antwerp in the village of Gheel, near the shrine dedicated to St. Martin of Tours. With Gerebern instructing them and offering the Sacrifice of the Mass, the group led virtuous lives, spending time in devotions and in acts of penance.

The King made a diligent search for his daughter, and followed her as far as Antwerp. From there he sent spies, who discovered the refuge of the fugitives. The clue by which they were traced was their use of strange coins—similar to those which the spies themselves offered in payment.

When the King finally confronted Dymphna, he at first tried to persuade her to return home with him—but he became enraged when he was again unsuccessful in his marriage proposal. When both Dymphna and her confessor attempted to explain the sinfulness of such a marriage, the King indignantly accused the priest of being the cause of Dymphna's disobedience—and ordered his immediate decapitation.

Deprived of the priest's support, Dymphna still remained steadfast. In a fury, her father ordered her execution. When his soldiers hesitated, the King himself severed his daughter's head with his own sword. Dymphna was barely fifteen years of age.

The two bodies were left exposed on the ground for days, since everyone was afraid to approach them because of the King. The bodies were eventually buried, in a humble manner, by the villagers.

The maiden was soon regarded as a saint, a martyr of purity and a champion over the wiles of the devil, who had brought her father to madness. In due time, those afflicted with lunacy sought her intercession and journeyed to her tomb in pilgrimage.

On account of the growing number of pilgrims, it was decided to give her body and that of her confessor worthier tombs inside the chapel. In digging for the remains, workmen were surprised to find the bodies in two coffins of white stone, of a kind unknown in the neighborhood of Gheel. This gave rise to the legend that the bodies had been reburied by angels after the original interment, since no one could remember their burial in white coffins. When the remains were exhumed, a red stone identifying the maiden was found on the breast of Dymphna.

During the Middle Ages, those who visited Gheel to invoke the saint were encouraged to make a novena of nine days at the shrine, while many afflicted persons participated in seven ceremonies called "penances." Among other practices, they were to attend Mass daily and recite prayers intended to exorcize the demons who were thought to have caused their illness. Until the eighteenth century the same prayers were said in Gheel for all the sick, without distinction between those believed devil-ridden and the mentally ill. During these prayers the red stone found on the remains of St. Dymphna was hung around the necks of the afflicted.

The relics of the saint are kept in a silver reliquary in a church that bears her name in Gheel, near Antwerp, Belgium. The church is believed to be situated over the saint's original burial place.

Today St. Dymphna is invoked worldwide for restoration of mental stability, as well as of religious fervor. She is the patroness of those suffering from mental and nervous disorders.

TWENTY

SAINT EDMUND, KING OF EAST ANGLIA

D. 870

ALTHOUGH he was almost fifteen years old at the time he was crowned King of East Anglia in the year 855, Edmund proved to be a model ruler from the first. He was eager to treat all with equal justice, and he performed his duties in a kind and Christian manner. He is said to have been as talented and successful a ruler as he was virtuous.

Edmund's character is well illustrated by Lydgate the Benedictine, who wrote in the fifteenth century that Edmund was "in his estate most godly and benign, heavenly of cheer, of counsel provident, showing of grace full many a blessed sign." In his eagerness to advance spiritually, Edmund retired for a year to his royal tower at Hunstanton and is said to have learned the whole Psalter by heart so that he might recite it regularly.

During the ninth century, the Northmen (or Danes) began to raid the coasts of England with greater frequency than they had formerly. The largest Danish invasion that ever took place occurred in the year 866 and began in Northumbria. When the invaders reached East Anglia, Edmund at first tried to resist by negotiating with the enemy. The *Anglo-Saxon*

Chronicle states that "in the year 867 a great army [of Danes] came to the land of the Angle race and took up winter quarters among the East Angles, and there they were provided with horses. And the East Angles made peace with them." The invaders then crossed the Humber and took York. Next they marched south into Mercia as far as Nottingham, plundering and burning as they went.

The preceding account of what took place is the earliest record available, but the traditional account of what took place is given by other historians, and in particular by St. Abbo of Fleury in his *Passio Sancti Eadmundi*. These reports are summarized by Butler in this manner:

> The barbarians poured down upon St. Edmund's dominions [in 8701], burning Thetford, which they took by surprise, and laying waste all before them. The king [St. Edmund] raised what forces he could, met a part of the Danes' army near Thetford, and discomfited them. But seeing them soon after reinforced with fresh numbers, against which his small body of soldiers was not able to make any stand, he retired towards his castle of Framlingham in Suffolk. The barbarian leader, Hinguar, had sent him proposals which were inconsistent both with religion and with the justice which he owed to his people. These the saint rejected, being resolved rather to die a victim of his faith and duty to God than to do anything against his conscience. In his flight he was overtaken and surrounded at Hoxne, upon the Waveney…Terms were again offered him prejudicial to religion and to his people, which he refused, declaring that religion was dearer to him than his life, which he would never purchase by offending God.

After restraining him with chains, Edmund's captors conducted him to Hinguar. When the party arrived there the same demands were made of Edmund, but these he again rejected, declaring that his religion was dearer to him than his life. This refusal was preliminary to a most cruel martyrdom.

After beating him with cudgels (short heavy clubs), the Danes tied him to a tree and cruelly tore his flesh with whips. During these tortures Edmund called upon the name of Jesus. Exasperated by his conduct, his enemies began to shoot arrows at him. This continued until his body is said to have taken on the appearance of a porcupine. When the enemy grew tired of this activity, Hinguar commanded his men to decapitate their victim. At the time of his death, Edmund was approximately thirty years old.

Edmund's first burial place was at Hoxne, but his relics were removed in the tenth century to the city of Beodriesworth, which was renamed St. Edmundsbury, or Bury St. Edmund. During another conflict with the Danes, the relics were taken to London, but were brought back to St. Edmundsbury three years later. During the reign of King Canute (d. 1035), the great Benedictine abbey of St. Edmundsbury was founded. The body of St. Edmund was the principal relic in the abbey church, which was the destination of many pilgrims—including King Canute and Henry VI. In 1465 a fire in the abbey caused substantial damage—from which it never fully recovered. The abbey was finally dissolved by Henry VIII in 1539. The disposition of the saint's relics is a matter of dispute.

In art St. Edmund is depicted with a sword and arrow, the instruments of his torture.

TWENTY-ONE

BLESSED EDWARD COLEMAN

D. 1678

B ORN in Suffolk, England, Edward was the son of an Anglican minister who provided for his son's education at the University of Cambridge. Afterwards, Edward became a zealous convert to the Catholic faith and secretary to the Duchess of York.

A contemporary Protestant chronicler refers to him as "a great bigot in his religion and of a busy head." But Edward Coleman was a man of talent and a dedicated Roman Catholic in a land which rejected the Pope and instead professed King Charles II as the head of the Church of England.

Edward's downfall came because of his friendly correspondence for many years with Père la Chaise, the French King's confessor, and his correspondence with other foreign friends. At this time, what became known as the Popish Plot, or the Oates Plot, appeared on the English scene. This was named for Titus Oates, a notorious informer, who intended to advance his own prestige and selfish interests by discovering alleged schemes of Roman Catholics to assassinate the King and restore the Pope's influence in England.

When Edward Coleman's foreign correspondence was

discovered, he was arrested as a participator in the "Popish Plot" and brought to trial at the Old Bailey on November 28, 1678. Edward was additionally charged with a plot to assassinate the King with the assistance of a foreign power. Although Edward engaged in a vigorous defense, proving that this charge and others were false, he was nevertheless convicted and sentenced.

On December 3, 1678, Edward Coleman was brought to the place of execution. His dying statement was recorded as follows:

> It is now expected I should speak and make some discovery of a very great plot. I know not whether I shall have the good fortune to be believed better now than formerly; if so, I do solemnly declare, upon the words of a dying man, I know nothing of it. And as for the raising of sedition, subverting the government, stirring up the people to rebellion, altering the known laws, and contriving the death of the king, I am wholly ignorant of it. . . . I am, as I said, a Roman Catholic, and have been so for many years, yet I renounce that doctrine which some wrongfully say that the Romish Church doth usher in to promote their interests: that kings may be murdered, and the like; I say, I abominate it.

After making other statements in which he continued to proclaim his innocence and to profess his allegiance to the Catholic faith, Edward Coleman recited some private prayers. The sentence was then executed. "He was hanged by the neck, cut down alive, his bowels burnt, and himself quartered."

Blessed Edward Coleman was beatified in 1929.

TWENTY-TWO

SAINT EDWIN

D. 633

A N UNHAPPY, unstable childhood characterized the early years of St. Edwin, who was deprived of his patrimony and obliged to wander from one temporary home to another. Additionally, he survived a number of threats and plots against his life.

It all began in the year 588 with the death of Edwin's father, Aella, king of Deira, England. At that time Ethelfrid, king of the Bernicians, seized Aella's kingdom and united all the Northumbrians into one monarchy. To secure his position over the territory that was to fall to Edwin, Ethelfrid placed the life of the three-year-old Edwin in jeopardy, making it necessary for the child to be quickly and secretly removed from the area. Edwin was moved from one friendly prince to another, his life being in continual danger from Ethelfrid's persistent efforts to destroy him. Eventually, when Edwin was a young man, he was accepted into the household of King Redwald of East Anglia.

When Ethelfrid learned the whereabouts of the exiled Edwin, he sent messengers to offer King Redwald a great sum of money to murder Edwin, but this was refused. Ethelfrid sent messengers a second and a third time, but Redwald continued to refuse until Ethelfrid threatened to invade his kingdom. According to the Venerable Bede:

> Redwald, either terrified by his threats or gained by his gifts, complied with his request and promised either to kill Edwin, or to deliver him up to the ambassadors. This being observed by a trusty friend of his [Edwin's], he went into Edwin's chamber, where he was going to bed, for it was the first hour of the night; and calling him out, discovered what the king had promised to do with him, adding, "If, therefore, you think fit, I will this very hour conduct you to a place where neither Redwald nor Ethelfrid shall ever find you."

Edwin thanked his friend but declined the offer, saying that Redwald had always proved to be a friend, and that "If I must die, let it rather be by his hand than by that of any other person." An unusual incident then took place. After his friend left him, Edwin remained outside, brooding over his misfortunes—when, as Bede reports, Edwin

> on a sudden, in the dead of night, saw approaching a person whose face and habit were equally strange, at which unexpected sight he was not a little frightened. The stranger coming close up, saluted him and asked him why he sat there alone and melancholy on a stone at that time, when all others were taking their rest, and were fast asleep?

The stranger then told him that he knew who Edwin was, why he grieved, and the evils which Edwin thought would happen to him at the hands of Redwald. The stranger then promised to deliver Edwin out of his anguish, to restore his kingdom to him and to persuade Redwald to preserve his safety if Edwin would promise to follow the directions of someone who would teach him the way to salvation. After

Edwin promised to comply, the stranger placed his hand upon Edwin's head and said, "When this sign shall be given you, remember this present discourse that has passed between us and do not delay the performance of what you now promise." The stranger then vanished. The Venerable Bede suggests that the stranger might have been an angel.

As the stranger had promised, Redwald "was diverted from his treacherous intention by the persuasion of his wife" and prepared to do battle to restore to Edwin his rightful claim to the throne. Redwald assembled a large army and marched against Ethelfrid, who was unprepared. During this battle, which took place in 616, Ethelfrid was killed on the field of combat. In an ironic development, Edwin, then about twenty-nine years old, was invited to reign as king—not only that portion of the kingdom which was bequeathed to him by his father, but also of the whole of Northumbria, over which his enemy had previously ruled. Edwin received the title of "bretwalda" and had a certain lordship over the other English kings.

We are told nothing of Edwin's first wife, but the Venerable Bede tells us that upon her death in 625, Edwin asked for the hand of Ethelburga, sister of Eadbald, the Christian king of Kent. The proposal met with some resistance, and Edwin was told that "It is not lawful to marry a Christian maiden to a pagan husband." The objection was overcome when Edwin gave his assurance that his wife would be free to practice her religion and that he would consider converting to her religion. Knowing that the word of the King was trustworthy, Ethelburga journeyed to Northumbria with her confessor, St. Paulinus, one of St. Augustine's fellow missionaries and the man who would be the celebrant at the royal wedding.

It seems that no king of that era, no matter how respected and beloved he might be, could relax his vigilance or be certain of a secure and peaceful reign. Edwin was no exception. One year after his marriage his life was again threatened, this time by Cuichelm, king of the West Saxons. Cuichelm sent an assassin named Eumer to stab King Edwin with a dagger which had been dipped in poison, "to the end that if the wound were not sufficient to kill the king, it might be performed by the venom." Eumer would certainly have killed Edwin if Lilla, Edwin's favorite minister, had not stepped between them to protect his monarch. In so doing, Lilla saved the King's life with the loss of his own.

During the same night, that of the attempted assassination, Queen Ethelburga gave birth to a daughter. King Edwin gave thanks to his idols for her safe delivery, but St. Paulinus told him that it was not the false gods that were responsible for the queen's easy and safe delivery, but rather it was the true God, whose Son was Jesus Christ. The King considered the matter and gave his consent for his newborn daughter to be consecrated to God. She was baptized on Whitsunday and was named Eanfleda.

Following the baptism, Edwin promised Paulinus that if God made him victorious over Cuichelm, who had ordered his assassination, and those who had conspired against his life, that he would himself become a Christian. He assembled his army and marched against Cuichelm, King of the West Saxons. Once again Edwin found cause to rejoice: His enemy was killed on the field of battle. Moreover, his army either killed or took as prisoners all those who had plotted against him. After this decisive victory Edwin abandoned the worship of idols and listened to the instructions of St. Paulinus. St. Bede reports that Edwin, a man of unusual wisdom, "sat much alone by himself, silent of tongue, deliberating in his heart how he should act and to which religion he should adhere."

Pope Boniface V, aware of Edwin's struggle in the matter, sent him an encouraging letter and a silver looking-glass. For the Queen, the Pope sent an ivory comb and a letter in which he asked her to use her powers of persuasion to influence the King in his decision.

St. Paulinus continued to instruct the King, but without any sign that Edwin would honor his pledge to convert if he were victorious over his enemy. But one day, while praying for Edwin, Paulinus approached him and placed his hand upon his head, asking him if he remembered the sign. Edwin suddenly recalled the stranger from the past who had also placed a hand on his head, telling him to remember the incident. Overcome with emotion and trembling, Edwin fell to his knees; but Paulinus, raising him up, told him kindly, "You see that God has delivered you from your enemies; and He offers you His everlasting Kingdom. Take care on your side to perform your promise by receiving His Faith and keeping His Commandments."

After overcoming the emotion of the moment, Edwin still had a spark of resistance; he told Paulinus that he would assemble his nobles and councilors to ask their advice—and that if they agreed, they too might join him in accepting the new Faith. During this meeting Coifi, the chief priest, declared with amazing candor that, by experience, it was manifest that their gods had no power: "No one has worshipped them more diligently than I, but others are more preferred and more prosperous than I am. If our gods were any good they would favor me, who have been more careful to serve them!" Another said that the short moment of this life is of little consequence if it is put in the balance with eternity. Others also spoke negatively of their gods and favorably of the new beliefs. Paulinus then addressed the assembly, after which Coifi applauded his words and asked the King to destroy the idols and to set fire to the pagan temples.

The promises Edwin had made, first to the stranger and then to Paulinus, were honored on Easter Sunday in the year 627 with his baptism in the wooden church of St. Peter. He had previously arranged for the building of this church; it has since been replaced by the present York Minster.

Following his baptism, Edwin became zealous for the conversion of his people, and to these he was an example of a devout and sincere convert. So many of Edwin's subjects now asked for baptism that the Venerable Bede tells how the King and Queen entertained Paulinus for five weeks at their royal Villa of Yeverin in Northumberland, with the saint being occupied from morning to night in instructing and baptizing the crowds that flocked to him. Of the King's family members, Paulinus baptized four sons, one daughter and one grandson.

Under Edwin the laws of the kingdom were much respected. As proof of this we are told that St. Edwin, concerned for the welfare of travelers, provided brass cups at springs which were located near frequently used roads. It is said that no man would dare touch these cups for any reason except for the purpose for which they were provided. As another example, Venerable Bede tells that "a woman with her newborn babe might walk throughout the island, from sea to sea, without receiving any harm."

For Edwin, peace did not last long. Once again an enemy threatened his life, this being the Welsh Chief Cadwallon, who marched against him with Penda, the pagan King of Mercia. King Edwin faced the enemy on the field of battle. During the conflict he was killed, together with his son Osfrid. The day was October 12, 633. Edwin was forty-seven years of age.

Since Edwin had died during a conflict with the enemies of the Faith, he was regarded as a martyr and as such was allowed by Pope Gregory XIII to be depicted in the English College Church at Rome. His relics at York Minster and at Whitby were held in great veneration.

TWENTY-THREE

SAINT EPIPODIUS AND SAINT ALEXANDER

D. 178

ONE year after the martyrdom of Sts. Blandina and Pothin in Lyons, France, the persecution of Marcus Aurelius continued to claim other victims. Among them were two young men, St. Epipodius and St. Alexander, who likewise suffered and died in Lyons. Epipodius was a native of that city, while Alexander was a Greek by birth. From their first studies together in the same school, they had become friends and together advanced in virtue. Both were Christians of good position and unmarried.

Betrayed by a servant who denounced them as Christians, Epipodius and Alexander became fearful. They had been friends of Blandina and Pothin, and knew of their sufferings and cruel death. They feared similar treatment when they learned of their own betrayal and impending capture. For this reason they journeyed to a neighboring town, where they hid themselves in the house of a poor widow. We are not certain exactly how long they were able to avoid detection, but eventually they were arrested. Still hoping to avoid a cruel death, Epipodius attempted to escape. In the process he lost a shoe, which was later treasured as a relic.

We are not told exactly what prompted a change, but after a three-day imprisonment Epipodius and Alexander showed exemplary courage by boldly professing their faith when questioned by the Governor. The two were then separated. Epipodius, the younger, was considered the weaker of the two and the one who might be more easily perverted. He was treated kindly at first, but when he refused to deny his faith he was struck soundly on the mouth. With bleeding lips, Epipodius continued to profess his faith. He was then stretched on the rack while his sides were torn with iron claws. To satisfy the people, who were clamoring for his death, the Governor ordered Epipodius to be beheaded.

Two days later Alexander expressed a fervent desire to join his friend, and he prayed fervently that Epipodius' brave martyrdom would encourage him in his trials. While stretched on a rack, he withstood a scourging by three executioners. With profound courage Alexander continued to profess his faith. His steadfastness so infuriated those who were inflicting the pain that he was sentenced to the ultimate punishment—crucifixion. Due to his extremely weakened condition, the martyr died the moment his mutilated limbs were fastened to the cross.

The triumph of these two martyrs is believed to have taken place in the month of April, in the year 178. Christians privately carried off their bodies and buried them upon a hill. There miraculous cures took place during a pestilence which afflicted the city of Lyons. The author of their *Acts,* Ruinart, attests to these miracles.

Unusual relics of these two saints included dust taken from their tombs—something which St. Eucherius, bishop of Lyons, first mentioned in his panegyric of the two martyrs. St. Gregory of Tours also attested to the benefits derived from this dust on behalf of the sick. In the sixth century, the bodies of the two martyrs were deposited with the body of St. Irenaeus under the altar of the Church of St. John. This church was later renamed for St. Irenaeus. The relics of St. Epipodius and St. Alexander were said to have been discovered, identified and solemnly translated in 1410. However, at the present time the Church of St. Irenaeus has neither a reliquary, tomb or statue in their honor.

TWENTY-FOUR

SAINT EULALIA
OF MERIDA

D. 304

A HYMN written by Prudentius at the end of the fourth century, along with St. Eulalia's *Acta* of a much later date, give us the particulars of the martyrdom of St. Eulalia, the most celebrated virgin martyr of Spain.

When the edicts of Diocletian were issued, by which it was ordered that all should offer sacrifice to the gods of the empire, Eulalia was a mere twelve years of age. The courage with which the martyrs rejected the edicts and died for the Faith so inspired the young girl that she too wanted to offer her life for her Christian faith. This desire for martyrdom troubled Eulalia's mother to such an extent that she took her daughter into the country. But during the night Eulalia left without telling her mother, arriving at Merida at daybreak.

When Dacian, the judge, entered the court to begin the daily session, Eulalia presented herself before him and declared that he should not attempt to destroy souls by making them renounce the only true God. Dacian was at first amused with the actions of the young girl and attempted to flatter and bribe her into withdrawing her words and observing the edicts. When she firmly renounced this tactic, Dacian then changed his attitude and showed her the instruments of torture, saying, "These you shall escape if you will but touch a little salt and incense with the tip of your finger."

What next transpired startled those in the courtroom. Eulalia at once threw down the image of the false god, trampled on the cake which had been laid for the sacrifice and spat at the judge. The sentence of the girl was quickly pronounced.

Two executioners seized her and took her to a place of torture, where they began to tear her body with iron hooks. As an added punishment for her actions, lighted torches were applied to her wounds. Quite unexpectedly, the fire from the torches caught Eulalia's hair, surrounding her head in flames. Stifled by the smoke and flames, Eulalia died. In his poem, Prudentius tells us that a white dove seemed to come out of her mouth and fly upward. Seeing this, the executioners became so terrified that they fled.

Eulalia's body was entombed by Christians near the place of her martyrdom. Later a church was built over the spot. Of this place Prudentius wrote in his hymn, "Pilgrims come to venerate her bones, and she, near the throne of God, beholds them and protects those that sing hymns to her."

The relics of the twelve-year-old martyr are now found in the Cathedral of Oviedo in a seventeenth-century chapel dedicated to her.

TWENTY-FIVE

SAINT FELICITAS AND HER SEVEN SONS

D. SECOND CENTURY

FELICITAS was a Christian woman of social importance who lived in Rome and served God in her widowhood by applying herself to prayer, fasting and works of charity. Through her prayers and edifying example she and her whole family were instrumental in turning many away from the adoration of false gods, leading them instead to adore the true God through joining the Christian faith.

Their success in this endeavor angered the pagan priests, who reported the matter to Emperor Antoninus, claiming that if Felicitas was not forced to venerate the gods, the gods would be so irritated that it would be impossible to appease them. To satisfy the priests, the Emperor sent an order to Publius, the prefect of Rome, to have the mother and her sons apprehended and brought to him.

Taking Felicitas aside, the Emperor attempted to persuade her to sacrifice to the gods—but when kind words did not impress her, he tried to frighten her with threats of bodily harm to herself and her sons if she did not comply.

Felicitas stood firm and refused to offend the true God by such an act. As her sons were being brought before the

Emperor, the brave widow exhorted them to remain firm in their faith. All seven refused to cooperate and were severely whipped. The Emperor then ordered that they be sent to different judges, who would order punishments as they deemed proper.

Januarius, the eldest son, was eventually scourged to death; Felix and Philip were beaten with clubs; Silvanus was thrown down from a steep rock; Alexander, Vitalis and Martial were beheaded, as was their mother, last of all.

Concerning the death of St. Felicitas, St. Augustine wrote:

> Wonderful is the sight set before the eyes of our faith. We have heard with our ears and seen with our minds a mother choosing for her children to finish their course before herself, contrary to the movement of human instincts. For all men would rather leave this world before their children, but she chose to die after them. . . . It was not enough that she had to look on; we are yet more astonished that she encouraged them...seeing them contend, she contended, and in the victory of each one she was victorious.

St. Gregory the Great also appreciated the sacrifice of the heroic mother. On the festival of St. Felicitas, November 23, in the church built over her tomb on the Via Salaria, he said that the saint

> having seven children, was as much afraid of leaving them behind here on earth as other mothers are of surviving theirs. She was more than a martyr, for seeing her seven children martyred before her eyes, she was in some sort a martyr in each of them. She was the eighth in order of time, but was from the first to the last in anguish, beginning her martyrdom in the eldest and finishing it in her own death...Seeing them in torments she remained constant, feeling their agony

by nature as their mother, but rejoicing for them in her heart by hope.

St. Gregory contrasts our faith against the heroic faith of this martyr and instructs us in the following manner:

> Let us be covered with shame and confusion that we should fall so far short of the virtue of this martyr. . . . Often one word spoken against us disturbs our minds; at the least breath of contradiction we are discouraged or provoked; but neither torture nor death was able to shake her courageous soul. We weep without ceasing when God requires of us the children He hath lent us; and she bewailed her children when they did not die for Christ, and rejoiced when she saw them die.

Alban Butler, the hagiographer, adds this counsel:

> Parents daily meet with trouble from disorders into which their children fall through their own bad example or neglect. Let them imitate the earnestness of St. Felicitas by forming to virtue the souls which God has committed to their charge, and with this saint they will have the greatest of all comforts in them, and will by His grace count as many saints in their family as they are blessed with children.

St. Felicitas was buried in the catacomb of Maximus on the Via Salaria, beside her son Silvanus. The crypt where Felicitas was laid to rest was later enlarged into a subterranean chapel, which was rediscovered in 1885. Still visible on the rear wall of this chapel is a seventh-century fresco which depicts St. Felicitas and her seven sons. Overhead is a figure of Christ bestowing on them the crown of eternal life. The relics are now found in the Church of Santa Susanna ("The Church of American Catholics" in Rome). Toward the end of the eighth century, the relics of the saint and her son Silvanus were placed in the crypt of this church, which is decorated with frescoes depicting scenes in the life of this holy mother and her courageous sons.

TWENTY-SIX

SAINT FLORA AND SAINT MARY

D. 851

ALL that we know of these two virgin martyrs was recorded by St. Eulogius of Cordova, Spain. Like the two women, he also suffered imprisonment and martyrdom during a persecution by the Moslems of North Africa, who had invaded Spain.

Flora was a Mohammedan in her early years by virtue of her father, but her mother secretly instructed the child in the Christian faith. After her baptism her own brother, a Moslem, vengefully betrayed her before the judge of the city. The magistrate had her scourged and beaten on the head until, in some parts, her skull was exposed.

Eulogius wrote, "I, wicked sinner that I am, knew her from the beginning of her sufferings; these hands of mine have touched the scars made by the whip on that lovely and noble head, from which the hair was torn out."

After these sufferings, Flora was released into the custody of her brother in the hope that he could persuade her to renounce the Christian faith. A short time later she escaped over a high wall and took shelter with a sister who lived in Ossaria. After a time the Moslems were not only persecuting

Christians, but were also inflicting punishments on those who concealed them. Flora's sister and her household were fearful that the poor girl would be betrayed and that they would suffer as a result. For this reason Flora was asked to leave. She then returned to Cordova and entered the Church of St. Acisclus to pray for guidance.

There she met the virtuous Mary, the sister of the deacon St. Valabonsus, who had died for the Faith a few days earlier. After much prayer and consideration, Flora and Mary realized that their arrest was inevitable and decided to make a courageous profession of their faith to the magistrate of the city. This they did. They were subsequently confined in a dungeon where no one had access to them except some wicked women who were sent to corrupt them. Of this effort Eulogius, who was in prison at the time, wrote to them:

> They threaten to sell you into a shameful slavery, but do not be afraid: no harm can come to your souls, whatever infamy they inflict on your bodies. Cowardly Christians will tell you that churches are empty and without the Sacrifice because of your obstinacy, and that if you will only yield for a time all will be well. But you may be certain that for you a contrite and humble heart is the sacrifice that pleases God most: you cannot now draw back and renounce the faith you have confessed.

Every effort was made to induce the girls to renounce their faith. Somehow Eulogius was able to visit the prisoners; he wrote, "I encouraged her [Flora] as best I could, bringing to mind the crown she had earned. Bowing low before her, I asked her prayers; and then, new heart put into me by all she had said, I left her angelic presence and went back to my dungeon."

During the afternoon of November 24, 851, Flora and Mary were beheaded after making the Sign of the Cross and bowing their heads to the sword.

During St. Eulogius' last visit with the two martyrs, they told him that they would intercede in heaven for his release and the release of his brethren. Five days after the virgin martyrs' execution, Eulogius was given his freedom. In *The Memorial of the Saints,* St. Eulogius attributes his deliverance to the intercession of the two saints. By means of his preaching, writings and example, he strengthened the Spanish Christians, especially when the persecution was intensified in 853. Six years later St. Eulogius was himself beheaded.

TWENTY-SEVEN

SAINT GENESIUS

D. C. 300

CONSIDERED to be the favorite comedian of his day, Genesius was the leader of a theatrical troupe that performed one day at Rome before the Emperor and a large audience. A professed heathen, Genesius performed a comedy routine that day which consisted of ridiculing the ceremonies of the Christian Church. He intended to amuse the Emperor by mocking the Sacrament of Baptism by performing a little skit in which he supposedly received the sacrament.

While Genesius acted the part of a dying Christian, a fellow actor, impersonating the character of a priest, approached Genesius and asked, "Well, my child, why hast thou sent for me?" There was a momentary pause—during which Genesius suddenly received the grace of conversion. Then, in all seriousness, Genesius replied, "I desire to receive the grace of Jesus Christ and to be relieved from the weight of my sins, which oppress me." The actor who pretended to be a priest continued the performance by pouring water over the comedian's head.

During this time Genesius is said to have had a vision of an angel who was surrounded by a heavenly light. Holding in his hand a book in which the sins of Genesius had been written, the angel immersed the book in the baptismal water and then showed it to Genesius. The sins had all been removed, and the book was perfectly white.

As the play progressed, Genesius was clothed in the white robe of the neophytes, after which certain players representing soldiers came to seize him and present him to the Emperor as a Christian. But when he was brought before the Emperor, he was no longer a comedian playing a part, but a true believer in Jesus Christ. He described for the Emperor the vision he had experienced and professed himself to be a Christian. At first the emperor was greatly amused, thinking the profession of faith to be a part of the play, but when he realized the seriousness of the situation, he became so irritated that he ordered Genesius to be severely beaten with clubs. After the beating Genesius was handed over to Plautian, prefect of the praetorium, who was to inflict torture in an effort to make Genesius renounce the Faith.

On Plautian's orders, Genesius was stretched upon the rack, torn with iron hooks and burned with torches. During these sufferings Genesius declared, "All possible tortures shall never take Jesus Christ from my heart or from my lips. My only grief is that I have so long persecuted His holy name, and have learned to adore Him so late." Genesius was then beheaded.

It should be mentioned that Genesius did not properly receive the Sacrament of Baptism during the performance, but he seems to have received baptism of desire, or at least baptism of blood at his martyrdom.

Genesius was venerated at Rome in the fourth century. A church built in his honor was repaired and embellished by

Gregory III in 741. In the Roman Church of Santa Susanna the relics of St. Genesius are found in the Chapel of St. Lawrence, which was added in 1585 by Pope Sixtus V (d. 1590).

The Church historian and theologian Ruinart (d. 1709) gives information on St. Genesius (who died between the years 285 and 303) in his monumental work on the lives of the martyrs which he called *Acta Primorum Martyrum Sincera et Selecta*. Based on authentic documents, it is said that "taken as a whole the collection is not surpassed even today."

TWENTY-EIGHT

SAINT HALLVARD

D. 1043

BECAUSE their father, Vebjorn, was a landowner and a merchant, Hallvard Vebjornsson and his brother Orm were considered persons of rank and honor. Thorny, Hallvard's mother, was related to St. Olav's mother. The family lived quite comfortably on their large estate, which was located on the side of the Drammenfjord which is approximately fifteen miles from Olso, Norway.

Hallvard was a Christian from childhood. Neighbors said that he was chaste, honest, religious, obedient to his parents and kindly to everyone. When the brothers were old enough, their father began to take them on his merchant travels. Hallvard was about thirteen years old at the time of his first voyage. It is not too surprising, then, since Hallvard was introduced so early to traveling abroad, that he was permitted to travel alone on matters of business while he was still an adolescent.

Accounts of two incidents that took place during this time have come down to us. We are told that once, when Hallvard's ship lay off the coast of Gothland, a rich young man came by to speak with the visitors from the north. Upon seeing Hallvard, he inquired as to who the young boy might be, since there was something remarkable about him. The rich young man told Hallvard, "I am certain that you are destined to do great things in your time." He invited Hallvard and all his companions to his home for a banquet and gave Hallvard rich gifts. We are told that this young nobleman of Gothland died as a martyr thirty years later. He is known as St. Botvid, the Apostle of Sodermanland.

The second incident that occurred during St. Hallvard's adolescence resulted in his early death.

First we must consider the punishment given in those days for stealing, which was considered a lamentable and despicable offense—so much so that no one had pity for a thief. A freeborn woman who had stolen was exiled; a bondwoman who had stolen suffered the loss of her ear for the first offense, the other ear for the second offense, and for the third offense her nose was cut off. The grim humor of the law allowed that "after that she can sniff and steal as much as she likes."

Hallvard's meeting with a strange woman came about one day when he left home to cross the Drammenfjord to transact business in the district on the other side. He was stepping into his boat when a woman came running toward him. She was terribly frightened and begged Hallvard to take her with him in the boat and row her to the opposite shore as quickly as possible. Hallvard helped her on board and had rowed only a short distance when three men came running to the shore from the same direction from which the woman had come. They boarded another boat and frantically rowed after Hallvard and the woman. In answer to Hallvard's question the woman acknowledged that she knew the men, but she explained that they accused her of stealing—a crime which she had not committed. Hallvard asked her if she were willing to prove her innocence through the ordeal by fire. She answered that she would do so, if only the men would spare her life.

When the boat gained on them the men asked Hallvard to surrender the woman, whom they wished to kill for the crime of breaking into the house of their brother. They claimed that she had "wrenched the bolt away which holds fast the boom across the door."

Having noticed that the woman was pregnant, Hallvard argued that it would require a man of considerable strength to do what they claimed she had done to gain entrance. With the poor woman huddled in the front of the rocking boat, Hallvard tried as best he could to defend her by presenting the inconsistencies of the accusation and by appealing to the men's sense of charity. But they were quickly losing patience.

Suddenly one of the men drew his bow and shot an arrow that struck Hallvard in the throat. They killed the woman also and buried her on the shore. Hallvard's body was thrown into the fjord with a millstone around the neck. Legend says that the body floated up, in spite of the millstone, and was buried in the church at Husaby.

Immediately, signs and miracles took place at Hallvard's grave, and he was acknowledged a martyr who had given his life in the defense of one of God's unfortunates.

Hallvard died in the year 1043. Years later his body was laid in a shrine and was moved to the new Christ Church in Oslo. The Catholic Church set May 15 as his feast day. Later, when Oslo became a bishopric, St. Hallvard was named patron saint of the diocese. It is said that his image has been incorporated in the arms of the city ever since. In art, the saint is pictured as a handsome youth holding a millstone.

TWENTY-NINE

SAINT HERMENGILD

D. 585

LEOVIGILD, the Arian king of the Spanish Visigoths, fathered two sons, Recared and Hermengild, by his first wife, Princess Theodosia. She saw to it that both sons were instructed in the Arian heresy, which their father also professed. Upon the death of Theodosia, Leovigild took as his second wife Goswintha, a fanatical Arian. This heresy denied the divinity of Christ and is considered to have been the most devastating of the early heresies. Eventually the heretics established their own hierarchies and churches.

In the year 576, Hermengild married the princess Indegundis, a zealous Christian. This marriage produced a clash in the family, with Goswintha resenting her daughter-in-law to the extent that physical violence was used in an attempt to make Indegundis abandon her Christian faith. The young princess, however, stood firm. Because of the patience his wife exercised with her mother-in-law and also due to her prayers—and the instructions from St. Leander, archbishop of Seville—Hermengild waited until his father's absence and then publicly renounced the heresy. He was welcomed into the Christian faith, receiving the imposition of hands and the anointing with chrism upon his forehead.

Leovigild, who had already been influenced against his son by Goswintha, was furious when he heard of his son's open profession of the Christian faith. He immediately deprived Hermengild of his title and called upon him to resign all his dignities and possessions. This Hermengild refused to do.

With the support of the Christians, Hermengild raised the standard of a holy war against the Arians. This endeavor was poorly planned, ill-equipped and lacking in manpower. The attempt proved to be a tragic mistake.

Because the Arians were powerful in Visigothic Spain, Hermengild sent St. Leander to Constantinople to obtain support and assistance. But the Emperor to whom the appeal was made died soon afterward, and his successor was obliged to use all available troops in an effort to resist an invasion of the Persians.

Disappointed with the unavailability of additional forces, Hermengild turned in desperation to the Roman generals who still ruled a strip of Spanish land along the Mediterranean Coast. They took his wife and infant son as hostages and made promises to Hermengild which they failed to keep. For over a year Hermengild was besieged in Seville by his father's troops, and when he could hold out no longer he fled to the Roman camp, only to be warned that those he had thought were his friends had been bribed by Leovigild to betray him.

Hermengild next made his way to the fortified town of Osseto, which he defended with three hundred men, until the royalist soldiers captured the town and burned it.

In desperation Hermengild entered a church and fell at the foot of the altar. Leovigild did not violate the sanctuary, but he permitted his younger son Recared, who was still an

Arian, to go to his brother with an offer of forgiveness, if he would submit and ask for pardon. Hermengild had no other recourse but to accept his father's offer. A reconciliation took place, and for the moment Leovigild waxed sentimental and restored to his son some of his former dignities.

Hermengild's stepmother, Goswintha, in the meantime had lost none of her former antagonism for Christians. As soon as the Arian father and his Christian son returned home, she was successful in estranging them once more. Hermengild was subsequently stripped of his royal robes, loaded with chains and imprisoned in the tower of Seville. (Another source claims he was imprisoned in Tarragona.) He was accused of treason and was offered his liberty if he would renounce his Christian faith. His reply was: "I am ready to lose sceptre and life rather than forsake the divine truth." For this statement he was transferred to a filthy dungeon, where he was subjected to various forms of torture. Praying fervently that God would sustain him in his sufferings, Hermengild added voluntary mortifications to what he already suffered at the hands of his persecutors.

St. Gregory the Great in *The Dialogues* (Book III, Chapter XXXI) tells what occurred next:

> When the solemn feast of Easter was come, his wicked father sent unto him in the dead of the night an Arian bishop to give him the communion of a sacrilegious consecration, that he might thereby again recover his father's grace and favor; but the man of God, as he ought, sharply reprehended that Arian Bishop which came unto him, and giving him such entertainment as his deserts required, utterly rejected him; for albeit outwardly he lay there in bands, yet inwardly to himself he stood secure in the height of his own soul.

The father, at the realm of the Arian prelate, understanding this news, fell into such a rage that forthwith he sent his officers of execution to put to death that most constant confessor in the very prison where he lay, which unnatural and bloody commandement was performed accordingly: for as soon as they came into the prison, they cave his brains with a hatchet, and so bereaved him of mortal life, having only power to take that from him which the holy martyr made small account of.

St. Gregory the Great continues by telling that as soon as the death of Hermengild was made known, miracles from heaven occurred. "For in the night time singing was heard at his body, some also reported that in the night burning lamps were seen in the place by reason whereof his body, as of him that was a martyr, was worthily worshipped by all Christian people."

St. Gregory also relates that the father was grief-stricken for having murdered his own son, but he never actually renounced Arianism. Yet, when he was on his deathbed, he recommended his son Recared to St. Leander, with the hope that the saint would convert his remaining son to the Christian faith. St. Gregory relates that

Recared the king, not following the steps of his wicked father, but his brother the martyr, utterly renounced Arianism, and labored so earnestly for the restoring of the Christian religion that he brought the whole nation of the Visigoths to the True Faith of Christ, and would not suffer any that was a heretic in his country to bear arms and serve in the wars. And it is to be admired that he became thus to be a preacher of the True Faith, being he was the brother of a martyr whose merits did help him to bring so many into the lap of God's Church, wherein we have to consider that he could never have effected all this if Hermengild had not died for the testimony of true religion.

After her husband's death, Indegundis fled with her son to Africa, where she died. Her son was then given to the custody of his grandmother Brunhilde.

Hermengild was venerated as a martyr soon after his death. Sixtus V, acting on the suggestion of King Philip II, extended the celebration of the martyr's feast, April 13, throughout the whole of Spain.

THIRTY

SAINT HYACINTH AND SAINT PROTUS

D. C. 257

POPE Damasus (d. 384) wrote an epitaph in honor of these two martyrs in which he calls Protus and Hyacinth brothers. They are also believed to have been slaves. The two martyrs were burned alive during the persecution of Valerian, in which St. Eugenia also perished.

The relics of Sts. Hyacinth and Protus, which were saved from the flames, were wrapped in a precious cloth and buried in the catacomb of St. Hermes on the ancient Salarian Way. During the fourth century, when access to the burial chamber became impossible, Pope Damasus had a staircase built and the place cleared so that devotees of the martyrs could easily reach the tombs. Centuries later the remains of St. Protus were transported to Rome; however, those of St. Hyacinth were not touched because the condition of the surrounding masonry niche indicated a hazardous situation. In 1845, though, Fr. Marachi discovered this niche intact. On the marble slab was the inscription: *D P III IDUS SEPTEBR. YACINTHUS MARTYR.* When the tomb was opened, only ashes and gold thread were found, along with what appeared to be parts of the charred bones of St. Hyacinth. It is said that a subtle perfume of roses arose from the bones upon their discovery.

The relics of the two saints are now found beneath the high altar of San Giovanni dei Fiorentini in Rome.

The facts mentioned above are all that we know for certain about these two martyrs. The various simple biographies which have come down to us are said to be fictitious. Since other authentic facts are not available, all we know is that these two brothers of lowly estate suffered and gave their lives for the Faith and were honorably buried in consecrated ground, apparently by those who were edified by their bravery and love for Christ and His teachings.

THIRTY-ONE

BLESSED JAMES BIRD

D. 1593

TWO years after the death of Ven. Laurence Mumphrey, who was martyred at the age of nineteen, James Bird died for the same cause, in the same manner, at the same age and in the same place.

James Bird was born in Winchester, England after Henry VIII had separated England from the Church of Rome. As the son of Protestant parents, James was reared as a Protestant, but on becoming convinced that the Catholic Church was the only true church, he received instructions and was baptized. He continued his studies at Douai College, but upon his return to England his zeal for his new faith caused him to come under scrutiny. He was soon apprehended and imprisoned. His charge was the same as that of Ven. Laurence: high treason. This accusation was made because James asserted that the Pope was the head of the Church on earth. James pleaded guilty to this charge and to the charge of being reconciled with the Church of Rome. His freedom was offered him if he would attend just one Protestant service. He steadfastly refused to compromise his conscience. When his father entreated him to make this one concession for the sake of his liberty, James replied that as he had always obeyed his father in the past, he would do so now—if by so doing he would not offend God.

After enduring the trials of his imprisonment, James was brought to the place of execution; there he was hanged, drawn and quartered. That is, he was hanged for a short time, then cut down alive and disemboweled, then his body was cut in four pieces. His head, like that of Ven. Laurence, was set on a pole atop one of the city gates.

Bishop Challoner, in his *Lives of Missionary Priests,* reports that one day while James' head was still upon the pole, his father passed by, and while viewing the head of his son, he thought the head seemed to bow as though in reverence. The father then cried out, "Ah! my son Jemmy, who not only living wast ever obedient and dutiful, but now also, when dead, payest reverence to thy father! How far from thy heart was all affection or will for treason, or any other wickedness!"

When James calmly met his martyrdom in 1593 he was only nineteen years of age.

THIRTY-TWO

BLESSED JAMES DUCKETT

D. 1602

AFTER receiving his education in Protestant schools, James Duckett was apprenticed in London, where he was given a book entitled *The Foundation of the Catholic Religion.* This book so shattered his belief in the reformed religion that he stopped attending the Protestant services in which he had been a regular participant.

Those with whom James lived noticed the change, found the book and carried it to Mr. Goodaker, the minister of St. Edmunds. He sent for James and asked him why he no longer attended (Protestant) services. James answered that he would continue to stay away from church until he had heard more convincing arguments in favor of the Protestant church than those he had previously heard. For this answer he was committed to Bridewell Prison. From there he was set free through his master's efforts, but he was soon accused again of not attending services. This time he was sent to Compter Prison. His master once again obtained his liberty, but being afraid of his association with James, his master released him from his apprenticeship.

Being free of this commitment, James was instructed in the Catholic faith and within two months was received into the Church by the venerable priest, Fr. Weeks, who was then a prisoner in the Gatehouse. From then on, James Duckett's life is described as having been virtuous and exemplary in all respects.

After living two or three years as a single gentleman, James married a good Catholic widow, Anne Hart, whom he supported by publishing and dealing in Catholic books. He did this not only for their own instruction and edification, but also for the assistance of their neighbors' souls. This occupation exposed James to many dangers and persecutions. He was apprehended and imprisoned so often that in his twelve years of married life he passed nine of them in prison.

James Duckett had one son, who afterward became the Prior of the Carthusians at Newport. Attributed to the son are the following details of James Duckett's last confinement:

> Peter Bullock, a bookbinder, after he had been condemned a twelvemonth, in hope, as many imagined, of obtaining his pardon, informed Lord Chief Justice Popham that James Duckett had had 25 of Father Southwell's Supplications to the Queen, and had published them. Upon this his house was searched at midnight but no such book found, nor sign thereof; yet they found the whole impression of Mount Calvary and some other Catholic books. However, James Duckett was apprehended and carried to Newgate, it being the 4th of March...Then evidence being called in, the same Peter Bullock accused James Duckett that he had some of Father Southwell's Supplications to the Queen, which he denied, having none of them. Bullock also avouched that he had bound for him divers Catholic books, and, amongst the rest, Bristowe's Motives which James acknowledged.

When the jury was asked to deliberate a verdict on the evidence given by only one witness, they found James not guilty. But Judge Popham stood up and told them to reconsider that Duckett had had Bristowe's *Motives* bound for him—a book that was controversial and contrary to the teaching of the new Anglican religion. The jury again deliberated, and this time found James guilty of a felony. The sentence of death was pronounced.

We are given a glimpse of the heartache suffered by James' wife on the day of his death, as described by their son:

> On Monday morning, the day designed for his death, his wife came to speak to him, which she could not without tears. He bid her be of good comfort, and said his death was no more to him than to drink off the candle which stood there ready for him. "If I were made the Queen's secretary or treasurer you would not weep. Do but keep yourself God's servant, and in the unity of God's Church, and I shall be able to do you more good, being now to go to the King of kings."

Peter Bullock, the bookbinder who had accused James Duckett in the hope of obtaining his own pardon, was not successful in this attempt. Rather, he found himself in the uncomfortable position of being in the same cart with James as they were both led to the place of execution. Concerning this situation, James Duckett's son continued:

> As he [James] was carried towards the place of execution, in the way his wife called for a pint of wine to drink to him. He drank, and desired her to drink to Peter Bullock, and freely to forgive him; for he, after all his hopes, was, in the self-same cart, carried also to execution. Being come to the place, and both he and Peter standing up in the cart, "Peter," saith he, "the cause of my coming hither, God and thyself knowest,

for which I, from my heart, forgive thee, and that the world and all here may witness that I die in charity with thee," he kissed him, both having the ropes about their necks. Then he said to him, "Thy life and mine are not long. Wilt thou promise me one thing? If thou wilt, speak: wilt thou die, as I die, a Catholic?" Bullock replied, he would die as a Christian should do. And so the cart was drawn from under them.

Thus Bl. James Duckett died at Tyburn, on April 19, 1602.

THIRTY-THREE

SAINT JAMES INTERCISUS

D. 421

DURING a great persecution of Christians in Persia, St. James served as a military officer and enjoyed considerable influence with King Ysdegerd I. To maintain this favor he renounced his Christian faith. Both his mother and wife, devout and steadfast Christians, were extremely grieved on learning what James had done for earthly influence. Upon the death of King Ysdegerd, they wrote to James in the following thought-provoking words:

> We were told long ago that for the sake of the king's favor and for riches you have forsaken the love of the immortal God. Think where that king now lies, on whose favour you set so high a value. He has returned to the dust, which is the fate of all mortals, and you cannot hope to receive the least help from him, much less protection from eternal torment. If you persevere in your crime, you yourself by the divine justice will receive the same punishment as your friend the king. As for us, we will have no more to do with you.

The letter so affected James that he repented, avoided the court, renounced the honors that had occasioned his fall and openly affirmed his faith in Jesus Christ.

His words were soon reported to the new king, who was

very annoyed. Realizing he would never be successful in persuading the saint to renounce his faith, the King threatened him with a lingering death.

After consultation with the council, it was decided that the criminal should be hung up and his limbs severed, one after another. When the dreadful sentence was made public, the city flocked to see this new form of punishment, while the Christians offered prayers for James' perseverance.

On reaching the place of martyrdom, James spent a moment in prayer and then offered his body to the executioners. At first they cut off his right thumb. When he did not abandon his faith, but continued his prayers, they cut off every finger, and then his toes. His limbs were then hacked off, joint by joint, and his thighs were torn from the hips. Lying a naked trunk, in indescribable agony, James continued his prayers until at last his head was struck from his body.

When the Christians secretly obtained the relics of the saint, they discovered that the body had been cut into twenty-eight different pieces. The author of the saint's *Acts,* who claims to have been an eyewitness, adds that following the heroic death, "We all implored the intercession of the blessed James."

The family name of St. James has been lost to us, but on account of the manner of his death, the name "Intercisus" was appended to that of St. James—"intercisus" meaning "chopped-to-pieces."

THIRTY-FOUR

SAINTS JOHN, ANTHONY, AND EUSTACE

D. C. 1342

KNOWN also by their Lithuanian names of Kumets, Kruglets and Nezilo, these three kinsmen of rank were employed as chamberlains in the household of Duke Olgierd, who ruled Lithuania from 1345 to 1377.

For a time they belonged to a sect of fire-worshippers, but after receiving instruction from a priest named Nestorius, they were baptized and became sincere Christians. They were conscientious in the performance of their religious duties, especially those regarding fasting and abstinence. Eventually they were cast into prison for their refusal to comply with the practices of paganism. After enduring many trials, they were condemned to death.

Anthony was hanged on January 14, and John, the eldest, was hanged on April 14. Eustace, the youngest, had to endure other tortures. He was beaten with clubs, his legs were broken, and the hair of his head was violently torn off because of his refusal to allow his hair to be shaved according to the custom prevailing among the pagans of the region. Eustace suffered and died at Vilna on December 13.

All three saints died about the year 1342 and were buried

in the Church of the Holy Trinity at Vilna, of which they have been regarded as the patrons since the time they were martyred. They are honored in the *Roman Martyrology* and also in that of the Russians.

THIRTY-FIVE

BLESSED JOHN SLADE AND BLESSED JOHN BODEY

D. 1583

IN THE *Stow Chronicle* of 1583 and in other works, mention is made of two men who were tried and condemned at the same time and for the same cause.

"John Slade, schoolmaster and John Bodey, Master of Arts, being both condemned of high treason for maintaining of Roman power, were drawn, hanged, bowelled and quartered," stated the *Stow Chronicle*. However, the two men neither suffered at the same place nor on the same day.

Bl. John Slade was born in Dorsetshire, England, and after receiving his education at New College, Oxford, he became a schoolmaster. His zeal in practicing his religion attracted the attention of the Protestants, who caused his arrest. He and Bl. John Bodey were arraigned together at Winchester and were there tried and condemned. Their case is different from many others who suffered for the same cause because they were tried twice and sentenced to death both times upon the same indictment. The reason for the death sentence was that they denied the Queen's spiritual supremacy and maintained that of the Pope.

Bl. John Slade was hanged, drawn and quartered at Winchester on October 30, 1583. He suffered and died for the Faith with great courage and virtue.

Bl. John Bodey was born in the city of Wells, in Somersetshire, in 1549. His father was a wealthy farmer and merchant of Wells. Like Bl. John Slade, John Bodey was educated at New College, Oxford, where he earned the degree of Master of Arts. For a time, he also studied canon and civil law.

On May 1, 1577 he arrived at Douay College in France, which served during that time as a refuge for those leaving England for the Catholic cause. Upon his return to England, his religious devotions and zeal for the Faith were noticed by the enemies of the Faith. He was apprehended in 1580 and, with Bl. John Slade, was first tried in the spring of 1583 for refusing to recognize the Church of England. Since the first trial was declared to have been unjust and illegal, the two were retried in August of the same year. They were again found guilty and were sentenced to the usual punishment— that of being hanged, drawn and quartered.

After the second trial, John Bodey wrote to Dr. Humphrey Ely on September 16 expressing the patience and constancy of himself and his fellow prisoners and asking "the good prayers of you all for our strength, our joy and our perseverance unto the end."

Some have suspected that John Bodey was married, because Bl. William Hart (d. 1583), also of Wells, in writing to his own mother mentioned that John Bodey was in prison with him and then asked to be recommended to "Mrs. Bodey and all the rest."

Challoner relates that, as John Bodey was being taken to

the gallows at Andover on the day of his death, November 2, 1583, "as he was drawn along the streets on a hurdle, his head being in danger of being hurt by the stones, an honest old man, pitying him, offered him his cap, in part to save his head; which Mr. Bodey with thanks refused, adding withal, that he was just now going to give his head, life, and all for his Saviour's sake."

Cardinal Allen informs us that when John Bodey was at the gallows, Mr. Kingsmell told him to confess the crime for which he was condemned so that the people would know the reason for which he was about to die. John Bodey then professed his obedience and fidelity to the Queen in all civil matters and added, "Be it known to all of you that are here present, that I suffer death this day because I deny the Queen to be the supreme head of the Church of Christ in England. I never committed any other treason, unless they will have hearing Mass or saying the Hail Mary to be treason."

It is said that John Bodey's mother, on hearing afterward about her son's death, made a great feast to which she invited her neighbors, rejoicing all the time that by his martyrdom her son's soul "was happily and eternally espoused to the Lamb."

Both John Slade and John Bodey were beatified in 1929.

THIRTY-SIX

BLESSED JOHN FELTON

D. 1570

JOHN Felton was from an ancient and wealthy Norfolk family and was related by marriage to the family of Anne Boleyn. His wife had been lady-in-waiting to Mary Tudor, the first daughter of Henry VIII, and was a personal friend of Elizabeth I, the King's second daughter. This was an unusual set of circumstances considering that all three—Anne, Mary and Elizabeth—were the principals during a turbulent time in English history.

On February 25, 1570, Pope St. Pius V issued the bull *Regnans in excelsis,* directed against Queen Elizabeth, who was at the time ostensibly a Catholic. By this bull she was declared excommunicate. Because she claimed to be the head of the Church of England, the Pope also declared that she should be deprived of the kingdom which she claimed and deprived of her subjects' allegiance. The Pope likewise accused her of sheltering heretics, oppressing and persecuting Catholics, and coercing her subjects into heresy and rejection of the Holy See, all of which was contrary to her coronation oath.

Early on the morning of May 25, the Feast of Corpus Christi, the citizens of London discovered that a copy of this bull of excommunication was fastened to the door of the house belonging to the Anglican Bishop of London. It had been put there during the night by Mr. John Felton, who lived in Southwark at a mansion built on the site of the former Cluniac Abbey of Bermondsey.

What we know of this incident was written in 1627 by G. Farrar, a priest known as a notary apostolic, who obtained his information from Felton's married daughter, Frances Salisbury. She tells us that

> the danger of such an employment, which my father took for an act of virtue, daunted him no whit. Whereupon promising his best endeavors in that behalf, he had the bull delivered him at Calais, and after the receipt thereof came presently to London, where being assisted with one Lawrence Webb, doctor of the civil and canon laws, he fastened it to the bishop's door.

Fearful of the punishment he would receive for such an audacious act, Dr. Webb at once left the country—but Mr. Felton would not think of leaving and calmly awaited the result of his action.

A great disturbance followed the discovery of the document, and searchers were sent to discover the culprit. When the chamber of a well-known Catholic attorney in Lincoln's Inn was being inspected, a copy of the bull was found. The attorney was arrested, and while being racked he confessed that he had received it from John Felton.

The next day the Mayor of London, the Lord Chief Justice, the two sheriffs of London and other officers presented themselves at the house of John Felton to arrest him. When Felton heard the knockings at his gate, he went to a window, and seeing the group ready to break down the gate, he called to them to have patience, saying he knew they had come for him. Felton's wife, who joined her husband at the window, fell down in a swoon at the sight of the officers.

Although John Felton admitted to what he had done, he was not brought to trial for three months. He was kept in the prison of Newgate and in the Tower and was three times racked in the hope that he would confess to a political intrigue with the Spaniards. But there had been no such intrigue. Felton had simply done what he thought was right and just and what he had to do to satisfy his conscience and principles; he had published the bull because it was a legitimate censure by the Pope for the Queen's religious offenses.

When he was finally brought to trial at the Guildhall on August 4, 1570, John pleaded guilty, forthrightly declaring the supremacy of the Holy See. By virtue of this confession and statement he was dragged four days later to St. Paul's churchyard, where a scaffold had been set up opposite the door on which the bull had been posted. Overcoming his great fear at seeing the instruments of his execution, John pointed at the Bishop's door, saying, "The Supreme Pontiff's letters against the pretended Queen were by me exhibited there. Now I am ready to die for the Catholic faith."

As a token of good will, he removed a valuable diamond ring from his finger and entrusted it to the Earl of Sussex for delivery to the Queen. This ring was of particular interest to the Lord Chief Justice, who had thought to claim it from the dead body.

After reciting the *Miserere* and commending his soul to God, John was hanged. The executioner would have let him hang until he was dead, but the Sheriff ordered that he be cut down alive. As John's heart was being torn from his body, his daughter Mrs. Salisbury heard him twice utter the name of Jesus.

John Felton was beatified with other English martyrs by Pope Leo XIII in 1886.

Eighteen years after the death of John Felton, his son Thomas Felton, who had been two years old at John's death, followed his father to martyrdom. Thomas, a Minim friar, refused under torture to reveal the names of priests; he was hanged at age twenty and was beatified in 1929.

THIRTY-SEVEN

SAINT JOHN RIGBY

C. 1570–1600

JOHN Rigby was the son of a Lancashire gentleman who had suffered a reversal of his wealth and holdings. Because of his father's situation, John Rigby was forced to seek whatever employment he could find, and he finally accepted a domestic position in the home of Sir Edmund Huddleston. His position in the household was awkward in that he was a Catholic living in a household whose members conformed to the Protestant religion. Because of the penal laws of the time, he occasionally attended Protestant services—a weakness which he afterward deeply regretted.

After a time, John confessed to a priest who was in the Clink Prison and was reconciled to the Catholic Church. Thereafter he led an irreproachable life and was successful in winning back several lapsed Catholics to the good graces of the Church.

John Rigby came under the focus of the authorities through his employment. His employer, Sir Edmund, had a daughter, Mrs. Fortescue, who was summoned to appear in court on the charge of having been reconciled to the Catholic faith. Because she was ill at the time, John Rigby was sent to the Sessions House of the Old Bailey to notify the court that she could not attend. While the judge was questioning him about Mrs. Fortescue, he turned his attention to John Rigby and inquired about his own religion. John Rigby frankly acknowledged that he was a Catholic and that he would not go to the church of which the Queen claimed headship. For this bold statement he was committed to Newgate Prison.

On June 19, 1600, during one of John Rigby's court appearances, an incident took place which many regarded as being miraculous. When John Rigby was standing before the bar, the judge saw that the prisoner had no irons on his legs; he sharply rebuked the keeper, who quickly brought a pair to the prisoner. John Rigby, taking them in his hands, kissed them, made the Sign of the Cross and gave them to the keeper. They were securely fastened on his legs and remained in place until John's appearance in court the next day. On that day, while John Rigby was standing in the Sessions House, the irons inexplicably fell off his legs. The keeper once again fastened them to the prisoner's legs, but after a short time they again fell off. The man who had twice secured them to the prisoner's legs was so amazed that they had fallen off a second time that he refused to put them on again.

It was then that John Rigby remembered that a Catholic maid called Mercy had told him that morning about a dream she had in which his irons had fallen off his legs. On being asked what he thought of the irons falling off his legs, which most thought to be miraculous, John Rigby answered that he hoped it was a token that the bands of his mortality would soon be loosed.

Two days later, when he was told that he would die that day, he answered, "It is the best tidings that ever was brought me since I was born." After bidding farewell to his fellow Catholics and asking for their prayers, John Rigby went to the yard, knelt down, made the Sign of the Cross, stood up, and with a smile he boarded the cart that would take him to the place of execution. On the way to St. Thomas' Watering, the place of execution, he was met by the Earl of Rutland and Captain Whitlock, who were on horseback. Stopping the cart, they asked him his name and other questions, which he answered in this manner: "My name is John Rigby, a poor gentleman of the house of Harrock, in Lancashire; my age about thirty years; and my judgment and condemnation to this death is only and merely for that I answered the judge that I was reconciled [to the Catholic faith], and for that I refused to go to [the Protestant] church."

The captain asked him to acknowledge the Queen as the head of the Church of England and thus save himself. This he would not do. After conferring with the sheriff's deputy about the matter in the hope of saving Rigby's life, the captain rode back to the cart and asked the prisoner, "Are you a married man or a bachelor?" "Sir," said John Rigby, "I am a bachelor, and more than that, I am a maid." After a few more words, the captain asked for John's prayers and then permitted the cart to move on to the appointed place.

Challoner, in his *Memoirs of Missionary Priests*, reports the brutality of John Rigby's death. After he had been hanged,

> the deputy commanded the hangman to cut him down, which was done so soon that he stood upright on his feet like to a man a little amazed, till the butchers threw him down. Then coming perfectly to himself, he said aloud and distinctly, "God forgive you. Jesus receive my soul." And immediately

another cruel fellow standing by, who was no officer, but a common porter, set his foot upon Mr. Rigby's throat, and so held him down that he could speak no more. Others held his arms and legs whilst the executioner dismembered and bowelled him. And when he felt them pulling out his heart, he was yet so strong that he thrust the men from him who held his arms. At last they cut off his head and quartered him, and disposed of his head and quarters in several places in and about Southwark. The people, going away, complained very much of the barbarity of the execution; and generally all sorts bewailed his death.

John Rigby was canonized in 1970. He is one of the Forty Martyrs of England and Wales.

THIRTY-EIGHT

SAINT JULIA

FIFTH CENTURY

WHEN the city of Carthage was taken by Genseric in 439, a noble maiden of the city named Julia was captured and sold as a slave to Eusebius, a pagan merchant of Syria. Setting aside her life of ease and privilege, Julia accepted her fate as the will of God and lived an exemplary life as a humble servant. She became so valuable to her master that he took her with him on a journey to Gaul, where he engaged in his profession as an importer of eastern goods. Having reached the northern part of Corsica, at a place now known as Cape Corse, their ship anchored. Eusebius went ashore to take part in a local pagan festival, while Julia remained on board, refusing to participate in the superstitious ceremonies, which she openly rejected.

When Felix, the governor of the island, was notified that Julia had dared to insult the gods by refusing to join in their festival, he confronted her owner, Eusebius, with this allegation. Eusebius admitted that Julia was his Christian slave, but he said that he overlooked her Christianity because she was a faithful, cheerful and conscientious servant whom he trusted with all he had. The Governor was so impressed with all that Eusebius claimed of his servant that he offered four of his best female slaves in exchange for her. To this offer Eusebius replied, "If you were to offer me all your possessions, they could not equal the value of her services!"

Later that night, while Eusebius was in a drunken slumber, the Governor took it upon himself to encourage Julia to sacrifice to the gods. As an inducement, he even offered her freedom from slavery if she would comply. Julia emphatically declined his proposal, saying that the only freedom she desired was to continue serving her Lord Jesus Christ.

Unaccustomed to such a bold reply by one in such a lowly position, the Governor viciously gave orders that she should be beaten on the face and that her hair should be torn out. After she underwent these sufferings, Julia was finally crucified.

We are told that monks from the Island of Giraglia rescued her body, which was later translated to different places. In the year 763 the body was removed to Brescia by the Lombard King Desiderius. The relic was placed by the Benedictine nuns in their church, which was consecrated the same year by Pope Paul I.

Julia is the Patroness of Corsica, which now claims some of her relics.

THIRTY-NINE

SAINT JULITTA AND SAINT CYRICUS

D. 304

WHEN the edicts of Diocletian were being strictly enforced against Christians, St. Julitta, a pious widow of Iconium, decided to seek safety in a more secluded location. Taking her three-year-old son Cyricus (Quiricus) and two maidservants, she went to Isauria, where she found the persecution raging under Alexander, the governor. From there the little party traveled to Tarsus, where Julitta was promptly recognized and imprisoned.

When she was called to trial, St. Julitta appeared, leading her child by the hand. As a woman of distinction, she owned property and many possessions—but when asked about these, she answered only that she was a Christian. For her refusal to cooperate, she was condemned to be racked and scourged.

While preparations were being made to rack Julitta, the child Cyricus was taken from her. The separation caused him to cry pitifully for his mother. In an effort to comfort him, the Governor took the beautiful child on his knee, but the boy would not be consoled. While his mother was being racked, he held out his arms to her and in a small voice kept repeating, "I am a Christian too." In a desperate struggle to be near his mother the child kicked Alexander and scratched his face. Furious at this behavior, the Governor seized Cyricus by the foot and threw him down, fracturing his skull. The boy died almost immediately from his injury.

Overcoming her distress at seeing her child killed before her eyes, St. Julitta prayed instead of giving in to grief; she thanked God for granting her child the crown of martyrdom. The Governor, still furious at the child and angry with the attitude of the mother, ordered that her sides be torn with hooks. After this was done, he ordered that she be beheaded and that her child's body should be cast out of the city with the bodies of criminals.

Following St. Julitta's execution in 304, her body and that of St. Cyricus were rescued by her two servants, who buried them in a field near the city. When peace was finally restored through the efforts of Constantine, the maids revealed the location of the graves, to the satisfaction of many Christians who came to venerate the two martyrs.

The feast day of Sts. Julitta and Cyricus was formerly observed on June 16. They are also mentioned in the calendars and menologies of the Greek and other oriental churches. Veneration of the two martyrs was common in the west at an early date, as is proved by the chapel dedicated to them in the Church of Santa Maria Antigua at Rome. In France, St. Cyricus is known as St. Cyr.

FORTY

SAINT JULITTA

D. 303

ST. JULITTA was a wealthy woman of Caesarea in Cappadocia who owned many farms, cattle and slaves. A dishonest but powerful man of the area, through intrigue, managed to acquire a considerable portion of her estate. When the matter could not be resolved amicably, Julitta found it necessary to seek protection under the law. When the man was brought to court, a decision in St. Julitta's favor seemed inevitable since the man could not produce a title to the holdings. In a desperate attempt to gain favor with the judge and thereby secure a right to the property, he denounced Julitta as being a Christian.

To test the charge, the judge ordered fire and incense to be brought into the court and commanded St. Julitta to offer sacrifice to Zeus. To this the saint bravely responded, "May my estates be ruined or given to strangers, may I lose my life, and may my body be cut into pieces, rather than that by the least impious word I should offend God. If you take from me a little portion of this earth, I shall gain Heaven for it."

With these words Julitta pronounced judgment on herself and the matter at hand, since earlier the same year the Emperor Diocletian had issued edicts against the Christians.

In these edicts he declared them impious and debarred them from all protection of the law and from the privileges of citizenship. In compliance with the edict of Diocletian and in retaliation for the audacity of her declaration of faith, the judge promptly gave the usurper full title to the lands he had maliciously claimed as his own, and condemned Julitta to death by fire.

Had St. Julitta denied her faith in Jesus Christ, her property would probably have been restored to her; instead, she smiled at her loss in such an edifying manner that the pagans were amazed to see a woman of her rank, age and fortune renounce everything for the sake of her faith.

Turning her back on that which the world holds dear, Julitta walked bravely into the fire and died after inhaling stifling smoke. Her body, which was untouched by the flames, was buried by fellow Christians.

What we know of St. Julitta, who died in 303, is given to us by St. Basil in a homily written about the year 375. Of the saint's body he says,

> It enriches with blessings both the place and those who come to it . . . the earth which received the body of this blessed woman sent forth a spring of most pleasant water, whereas all the neighboring waters are brackish and salt. The water preserves health and relieves the sick.

The feast day of St. Julitta was formerly observed on July 30.

FORTY-ONE

SAINT LUCIAN AND SAINT MARCIAN

D. C. 250

THE history of these martyrs is preserved to us in both Latin and in Syriac; the Greek text, which is probably the original, has been lost.

We are told that both Lucian and Marcian applied themselves to the study and practice of black magic. When they attempted to effect their charms on a Christian maiden, the evil spirits were defeated by the Sign of the Cross. This inability to apply their black magic is said to have converted them. Having received the gift of faith, they publicly burned their books of black magic and devilish materials in the city of Nicomedia.

After receiving baptism, Lucian and Marcian distributed their possessions among the poor and retired into solitude to practice mortification and prayer. Later they made frequent journeys to preach Christ to the Gentiles in order to gain souls for the Kingdom of Heaven. But after the edicts of Decius against the Christians were published in 250, the two were apprehended and brought before the Proconsul Sabinus, who asked Lucian by what authority he presumed to preach Jesus Christ. Lucian replied, "Every man does well to endeavor to draw his brother out of a dangerous error." When Marcian concurred in this statement, the judge commanded that Lucian and Marcian be cruelly tortured. To this they remarked that while they had worshiped idols and had committed many crimes and had made open profession of practicing black magic without incurring any difficulty, they were being punished for being good Christian citizens. At this, Sabinus condemned them to be burned alive.

The two went joyfully to the place of execution, singing hymns of praise and thanksgiving to God. "We are ready to suffer," they said, "but we will not renounce the true God, lest we be cast into a fire which will never be quenched." Lucian and Marcian were martyred in Nicomedia around the year 250.

FORTY-TWO

BLESSED MARCEL CALLO

1921–1945

O N THE feast of the Immaculate Conception, December 8, 1921, Marcel Callo, who was two days old, was baptized in the church of Notre-Dame de Bonne Nouvelle at Rennes, France.

Marcel's father was an employee of the Bridge and Streets Department of the city, but because of the responsibilities of raising nine children, it was difficult at times for Marcel's parents to provide all that was necessary for them.

While Marcel was still a child he was described as having been a leader, always happy, frank and open. He liked to organize and to express and defend his ideas, but when he was not pleased he would show his displeasure by a movement of the shoulder. Something of a perfectionist, Marcel liked everything to be in order, but he understood that he had to make concessions since he was not always correct.

As an older child of the family, Marcel was expected to help in the care and management of the household. He willingly helped his mother by washing the dishes, straightening the house, and by helping to wash and dress his younger brothers and sisters. Everything was easy for him, and he did his chores with care and in good spirits.

Marcel attended St. Anne School at Rennes and received a certificate after completing his primary studies. At the age of almost thirteen he was apprenticed to a printer. He was proud not only to support himself, but also to help in the support of his family. Like all the young people in the area, he gave all his salary to his mother, who in turn gave him what he needed for his expenses. He loved his trade and was proud to work with his hands. He once wrote that, "work assures us of the necessities of our existence and is for us a source of merit for the other life."

At least one difficulty arose during his apprenticeship, that of his fellow workers telling improper stories and using vulgar language. For this reason Marcel preferred the company of his comrades in an organization known as the JOC, *Jeunesse Ouvriere Chretienne* (Young Christian Workers). His friends in this organization corresponded more to his ideals and behavior. Under the inspiration of Pere Cardijn and Pere Guerin, who were its founders, the JOC provided instruction in the Catholic faith, good fellowship and wholesome activities.

His friends in the JOC later described Marcel as having been "dynamic, very cheerful...he knew how to laugh and how to make people laugh. He was an excellent friend." Another friend said, "Marcel possessed a joyful character, always happy and always very Christian." Another reported, "I always thought he had a good sense of humor. He was alive, dynamic and had the stuff of a leader." These friends also revealed that Marcel liked to wrestle, play football, ping pong, cards and bridge.

In 1941, when Marcel was twenty years old, he met and

fell in love with Marguerite Derniaux. Unlike his fellow workers who tended to degrade women, Marcel preferred the ideal behavior of his JOC friends. As he once said,

> I am not one to amuse myself with the heart of a lady, since my love is pure and noble. If I have waited until I was 20 years old to go out with a young lady, it is because I knew that I wanted to find real love. One must master his heart before he can give it to the one that is chosen for him by Christ.

It was almost a year later, in August of 1942, that Marcel declared his love, and it was four months later that he "suffered the embarrassment" of their first kiss. As his fiancée later wrote, "That day I was celebrating the completion of the training for my work. After Mass he kissed me for the first time. He had wanted to delay this gesture in order to thank God that we knew each other."

Four months later, they imposed on one another a rule for the spiritual life. This included the recitation of the same prayers, the frequent assistance at Holy Mass and the reception of the Holy Eucharist.

Marcel's orderly life of work and prayer was interrupted on March 8, 1943, when World War II touched the city of Rennes. On that day the city suffered a terrible bombardment. The train station and the streets around it were destroyed. Since Marcel worked close by, he and his worker friends went about helping those who were injured. When he noticed that the place where his sister, Madeleine, worked was leveled, Marcel dug under the debris and eventually discovered her body. It is reported that he fought the pain of his sorrow to tell his parents and family the terrible news.

What he feared for a long time eventually presented itself in the form of an order to report to the STO, *Service du Travail Obligatoire* (Service of Obligatory Work) in Germany. With France occupied by the Germans, young men were forced to report for work in Germany. Failure to do so would result in the arrest of a man's family.

Because of the recent death of his sister, Marcel delayed in telling his family of his imminent departure. An aunt to whom he confided his secret told him that she knew he would greatly benefit his friends. To this Marcel responded, "Yes, Aunt, I will do everything possible to do well because you know that it is not as a worker that I leave, but as a missionary."

Eleven days after his sister's death, Marcel left on a five-day trip to Zella-Mehlis, Germany. There he reported to a factory that made rockets which would be used against the French people. Although Marcel lived in a barracks and was forced to work, he and his companions were not considered to be prisoners. They had the freedom to come and go, and could participate in various activities.

Being far from his family, Marcel missed the first Mass of his newly ordained brother and the First Holy Communion of his little sister. Probably as a result of homesickness, Marcel suffered for three months from discouragement and had to fight against a terrible depression. During this time Marcel wrote that in Zella-Mehlis there was no Catholic church, but he was able to find a room where Holy Mass was offered on Sundays. This, he said, was a great comfort to him. In writing to his family he described his feelings and his need for consolation, and reported that, "finally Christ reacted. He made me to understand that the depression was not good. I had to keep busy with my friends and then joy and relief would come back to me."

Marcel began almost at once to restore good morale and hope among his deported friends. He organized a team of his Christian workers and had matches of bridge, cards, sports and other activities. He also organized a theatrical group which performed small plays. Around this time he wrote, "I believe I am still in Rennes in full activity. I give much and I receive much in return. When I do good things for others I am satisfied."

He continued to organize these activities with a holy deliberation despite suffering from painful boils, headaches and infected teeth which he said often transformed his head into a balloon. He also endured these sufferings while working more than eleven hours a day.

For his French comrades, Marcel was able to arrange for a solemn Holy Mass to be celebrated in their language. In a letter home, Marcel wrote:

> We had our first French Mass this morning. The result is that I am happy...it was a successful beginning. What enthusiasm! . . . We sang with one voice and we chanted the Credo. For us it was magnificent. . . . At the end I addressed a few words, then we prayed for all the ones we left in France and for all our friends working in Germany. All the people were very pleased. . . . They came to congratulate us and asked us for a French Mass every month. I am very happy to arrive at that result.

Eventually, Marcel's religious activities were brought to the attention of the German officials. This prompted Marcel's arrest on April 19, 1944. While Marcel was being taken away, Joel Poutrel, one of Marcel's friends, demanded a reason for the arrest. The agent of the Gestapo responded, *"Monsieur est beaucoup trop catholique"*—"Monsieur is too much of a Catholic." Marcel appealed to his friend: "Please write to my parents and to my fiancée that I am arrested for Catholic action."

During his interrogation, Marcel admitted that he was engaged in Catholic activities and that he knew this was forbidden in Germany. He was taken to the prison in Gotha, where he continued his life of prayer and his concern for his companions. It is believed that Marcel received his last Holy Communion during his stay at Gotha. Consecrated Hosts were secretly brought into the prison and were confided to a JOC friend, Henri Choteau, who kept them in a box for distribution. In a small journal that Marcel kept in prison he wrote, "16 July . . . Communion . . . immense joy."

After he was officially accused of participating in Catholic activities among his French friends, an activity regarded as harmful to the German people, Marcel was moved on October 24 to the prison at Mathausen. He was to suffer there for five months. In spite of sickness, he inquired about the needs of his companions, and encouraged them by saying, "It is in prayer that we find our strength."

Marcel suffered from general weakness, fever, swelling, bronchitis, malnutrition and dysentery. It is said that he never complained and that he "expired softly like a lamb." He died on the feast of St. Joseph, March 19, 1945, exactly two years from the day he left France for Germany.

Before Marcel left France his fiancée had told him, "You will be a martyr." Marcel Callo had replied, "I will never be good enough for that." But apparently the Catholic Church thought otherwise, since Marcel was beatified by Pope John Paul II on October 4, 1987. Beatified during the same ceremony were two Italian martyrs, Antonia Mesina, who died in 1935, and Pierina Morosini, who died in 1957.

FORTY-THREE

SAINT MARCELLUS

D. 298

S T. MARCELLUS was one of the martyrs who suffered before the outbreak of the great persecution of Diocletian in the year 303. The particulars of his passion are preserved in existing documents. A translation of Marcellus' *Acts* reads as follows:

> In the city of Tangier, during the administration of Fortunatus as governor, the time came for the birthday of the Emperor. When everyone was feasting and sacrificing, a certain Marcellus, one of the centurions of the Trajan legion, considering the banquet to be heathen, cast away his soldier's belt in front of the standards of the legion which were then in camp, and testified in a loud voice, saying: "I serve Jesus Christ, the Eternal King." He likewise cast away his vine switch [the distinctive badge of a centurion] and his weapons, adding, "Henceforward I cease to serve your emperors, and I scorn to worship your gods of wood and stone, which are deaf and dumb. If such be the terms of service, that men are forced to offer sacrifice to gods and emperors, behold, I cast away my vine switch and belt, and I renounce the standards and refuse to serve."
>
> Everyone was bewildered at hearing such things; they laid hold of him and reported the matter to Anastasius Fortunatus, the Commander of the legion, who ordered him to be cast into prison. When the feasting was over, he gave

orders, sitting in council, that the centurion Marcellus should be brought in.

Fortunatus questioned Marcellus, but the saint only replied that he rejected the gods and served only Jesus Christ, the Son of God. To this Fortunatus replied that he could not overlook such rash conduct, and he referred the matter to Aurelius Agricolan, deputy for the Prefects of the Guard.

On October 30 at Tangier Marcellus was brought into court before Agricolan. The charges against him were outlined in a letter from Fortunatus, which was read aloud:

> From Fortunatus to you, my lord. This soldier, having cast away his soldier's belt, and having testified that he is a Christian, spoke in the presence of all the people many blasphemous things against the gods and against Caesar. We have therefore sent him on to you, that you may order such action to be taken as Your Eminence may ordain in regard to the same.

Agricolan then questioned Marcellus about his rank as centurion and his actions the night of the celebration. Assured that the charges against him were accurate, Agricolan gave his verdict:

> The actions of Marcellus are such as must be visited with disciplinary punishment. Marcellus, who held the rank of centurion of the first class, having admitted that he has degraded himself by openly throwing off his allegiance, and having besides put on record, as appears in the official report of the Governor, other insane expressions, it is our pleasure that he be put to death by the sword.

After begging for God's blessing upon Agricolan, Marcellus was subsequently beheaded. The year was 298.

FORTY-FOUR

SAINT MARGARET CLITHEROW

(ST. MARGARET OF YORK)

1556–1586

CONSIDERED to be the first woman to have died under the religious suppression of Queen Elizabeth, Margaret was born in 1556 and lived all her life in the city of York. She was the daughter of Thomas Middleton, a wax-chandler (maker and seller of candles). He was a man of means and of some importance in the community, since he held various civic positions and for a time was a member of the Common Council. Five months after his death his widow married Henry May, who took up residence with the family at the Middleton house in Davygate.

Margaret lived with her mother and stepfather for four years, until the age of fifteen. Then she married John Clitherow, a grazier and butcher who, as her father had been, was wealthy and held a number of civic positions. There is every indication that Margaret's early married life was happy. Three children joined the family: two boys, Henry and William, and one daughter, Anne.

Margaret had been raised a Protestant. In the manner of

girls of her class, she was taught from childhood how to run a household, but not how to read and write. Two or three years after her marriage she became a Catholic, because, as her confessor wrote of her, she "found no substance, truth nor Christian comfort in the ministers of the new church, nor in their doctrine itself, and hearing also many priests and lay people to suffer for the defense of the ancient Catholic faith." Margaret's husband did not object to his wife's conversion, but he himself remained a faithful member of the new religion of which Queen Elizabeth professed leadership.

At first, Margaret freely practiced her faith and worked toward reconciling many to the Catholic Church. She became more cautious, though, when laws against Catholics were enacted and strictly enforced. Fines were initially imposed upon Mr. Clitherow for his wife's continued absence from Protestant services; later, for her continued absence from these services, she was imprisoned in York Castle. Between the years 1577 and 1584 Margaret was imprisoned several times. The second time she was seized and imprisoned, she was released because she was expecting a child. In 1584 she was imprisoned for eighteen months.

The conditions in the prison were unbearable. Records from that time reveal that the cells were dark, damp and infested with vermin, so that many died during their confinement. Margaret made the best of her condition by regarding her imprisonment as a time of prayerful retreat. She also used the time in learning how to read, and she returned to her home with habits of prayer and devotion which had been unfamiliar to her from her Protestant upbringing. She also began to fast four times a week, a practice she continued after her release. Her devoted husband once stated that he found but two faults in his good wife: She would not accompany him to the Protestant church, and she fasted too much.

During this time, Cardinal Allen had been conducting a seminary at Douai, France for the purpose of training young priests who would return to their native England to minister to those who had remained loyal to the Catholic faith. When these priests returned from Douai, Catholic life began to revive in the city and the shires. Finally a law passed in 1585 made it high treason for any Englishman who was ordained a priest since the first year of Elizabeth's reign to remain in the kingdom; and it was a felony for any person to harbor or relieve a Catholic priest. By these statutes it was only necessary to prove that a man was a Catholic priest, whether English or not, in order to condemn him to a cruel death—and a similar punishment was reserved for those who aided him.

We are not certain when Margaret began to conceal priests in her home, but when warned of the great risk she was inviting by accepting all the priests who came to her for sanctuary, she replied, "By God's grace all priests shall be more welcome to me than ever they were, and I will do what I can to set forward God's Catholic service." Margaret had in her home a secret hiding place with a passageway through which priests could hide or escape to the outside of the building. Here Frs. Thompson, Hart, Thirkill, Ingleby and many others took refuge. The place was apparently cramped and uncomfortable, since we are told that the entrance was "painful to him that was not acquainted with the door, by reason of the straitness thereof, and yet large enough for a boy."

Whenever a priest was visiting, Margaret arranged for the

Catholics of the area to attend Holy Mass. Fr. John Mush, her confessor and first biographer, wrote of Margaret that

> She had prepared two chambers, the one adjoining to her own house, whereunto she might have resort any time, without sight and knowledge of any neighbours. . . . The other was a little distant from her own house, secret and unknown to any but to such as she knew to be both faithful and discreet. . . . This place she prepared for more troublesome storms, that God might yet be served there when her own house was not thought so safe, though she could not have access to it every day as she desired.

Accounts of her contemporaries reveal that Margaret was witty, happy and charming. Neighbors commented on her pleasing appearance. They noted that she spoke always in a low voice and enjoyed a simple diet of rye bread, milk, pottage and butter. Like a true Yorkshire woman, she was careful about the neatness and cleanliness of her home, which was located in an area called The Shambles. Being a woman of some means, she had a number of servants. These she treated kindly, but she did not hesitate to correct them when their work was not properly completed—and she often worked beside them to show them how to execute their chores properly.

Margaret was also a capable businesswoman, who often helped in her husband's butcher shop located near their home. She was careful that the prices she asked for her husband's wares were fair and just. "In buying and selling her wares she was very wary to have the worth of them, as her neighbors sold the like, as also to satisfy her husband, who committed all to her trust and discretion." Mindful of her husband's many responsibilities, she often urged him to close the shop with its many concerns and instead to sell only on the wholesale level, which was less troublesome.

Everyone loved Margaret, we are told. Rev. Mush recorded that her friends "would run to her for help, comfort and counsel" and he told how "with all courtesy and friendship she would relieve them." Her neighbors respected her, and even though many were of the Protestant faith, they shielded her activities and warned her of danger. Her servants, who also knew of her illegal harboring of priests, loved her and were careful to guard her secret.

She was consistent in the practice of her faith, beginning every day with an hour and a half devoted to private prayer and meditation. If a priest was available, Holy Mass followed. Margaret regularly confessed, and although she was not an educated woman, she had learned to read during her imprisonments and often read the Holy Scriptures, the works of Thomas à Kempis and Perrin's *Exercise*. She had also learned, probably during her imprisonment, the whole of the *Little Office of Our Lady*.

When her son Henry came of age, Margaret obtained the permission of her husband to send him to Douai so that he might receive a Catholic education in the seminary that had been established to train missionary priests.

Sending a son or daughter outside the kingdom to receive a Catholic education was considered a crime, and as soon as the council learned of it, John Clitherow was ordered to appear before them for questioning. Since the Clitherow house had been marked as a rendezvous for missionary priests who ministered to the Catholic inhabitants of the city, and because the authorities had learned of the Clitherows' son's absence from the kingdom, a retaliation of some sort was expected.

On March 12, 1586, while John Clitherow was testifying before the council and Margaret was busy with her household concerns, two sheriffs of the city, accompanied by other men, entered the Clitherow house to search it. Nothing suspicious was found at first, but on opening the door to a remote room, the men found some children of the neighborhood who were being taught by a schoolmaster named Stapleton, whom they mistook for a priest. In the confusion that developed, Stapleton escaped through the secret room. Another account tells that Fr. Mush, Margaret's confessor, and Fr. Ingleby were also in the house at the time—but if so, they too escaped.

An eleven-year-old boy who was then living with the family was terrorized into revealing the secret hiding place. No one was found in the secret place, but in a nearby cupboard the authorities found church vessels, books and vestments that had been used during Holy Mass. The articles were taken as evidence and Margaret was arrested, together with all who were found in the house. The others were soon released, but Margaret was taken to the Common Hall for questioning and was then imprisoned in the castle. After being reassured that family members had been released and were safe, her good spirits returned and she promptly began to help the thirty-five women who were imprisoned with her.

During Margaret's next court appearance, the charges against her were revealed. These included the claim that she harbored and maintained priests who were working in opposition to the Queen's new religion. When the judge asked her whether or not she was guilty, Margaret replied that she had never harbored enemies of the Queen. Then, following the procedure of the court, Judge John Clinch asked her how she wished to be tried. Instead of the accepted reply, "By God and the country," Margaret replied, "Having made no offense, I need no trial." The vestments that had been found in her home during the raid were presented in evidence, but still Margaret refused to agree to a trial. Judge Clinch made every effort to get her to plead. At the same time his fellow judge, Francis Rhodes, who later had a part in the condemnation of Mary Queen of Scots, began to insult Margaret. "It is not for religion that thou harbourest priests," he called at her, "but for harlotries."

Knowing that she would die regardless of her answer, Margaret was also aware that during a trial, her children, servants and friends would be called as witnesses and would either lie to save her and commit perjury and sin, or if they testified truthfully, would bear the burden of having caused her death. She therefore repeatedly rejected a trial and steadfastly refused to acknowledge the Protestant church of Queen Elizabeth. The council was then forced to pronounce the sentence which English law decreed for anyone who refused to plead and be tried by a jury: *peine forte et dure,* that is, that she should be pressed to death. Margaret accepted the sentence calmly and thanked God that she would suffer for the sake of the Catholic faith.

When John Clitherow heard of the sentence passed on his wife, "He fared like a man out of his wits and wept so violently that blood gushed out of his nose in great quantity." He reportedly said, "Let them take all I have and save my wife, for she is the best wife in all England and the best Catholic, also."

Margaret was then confined in John Trew's house, where

she found no peace because of the various people who visited her, trying in vain to make her acknowledge the new religion and thus gain her liberty. Even her stepfather, Henry May, who had been elected mayor of York, tried to win her over. She was not allowed to see her children and only once saw her husband, and then in the presence of a guard.

The date set for her punishment was March 25, which was also Lady Day (the Feast of the Annunciation). The evening before she was to suffer Margaret sewed her own shroud, and during the night she prayed. She had already sent her hat to her husband, "in sign of her loving duty to him as head of the family," and she had dispatched her shoes and stockings to her twelve-year-old daughter, Anne, "signifying that she should serve God and follow in her mother's steps."

At eight the next morning, March 25, 1586, female attendants helped to robe Margaret in the linen garment she had made. Surrounded by the officers of the law and by her executioners, she was then led to the place of martyrdom, only a few yards from where she had been imprisoned. To reach this place she passed through a large crowd of people who had congregated to see the strange sight of a woman led to slaughter. "All marveled to see her joyful, smiling countenance." Arriving at the place, she knelt down and with a strong voice she prayed for the Pope, cardinals, clergy, Christian princes, and especially for Queen Elizabeth, that God would return her to the Faith and save her soul.

After Margaret lay down upon the ground, a sharp stone was placed under her back—and when she had extended her arms in the form of a cross, her hands were bound to posts on either side. A slab of wood the size of a door was laid over her,

and weights were dropped upon it. With her bones breaking at every additional weight placed upon her, Margaret did
not cry out in pain. Instead, her last words as the weight was
increased were, *"Jesu, Jesu, Jesu,* have mercy upon me." Her
torment lasted approximately a quarter of an hour. We are
told that her body remained in the press for six hours. At the
time of her death, Margaret was thirty years of age.

Margaret's crumpled body was taken by the executioners
to a secret burial place. Later, when her remains were found
by her Catholic friends, they were given a proper burial,
although the place is now unknown. One of her hands was
kept, and this is found in a crystal vessel at Bar Convent,
York, which is now a museum.

The martyr's daughter, Anne, inspired by the life and
death of her mother, became a nun at Louvain; her two sons,
Henry and William, both became priests.

Nearly four hundred years after her death, on October
25, 1970, Margaret was declared a saint by Pope Paul VI
before a crowd estimated at fifty thousand in St. Peter's
Basilica, Rome.

In the city of York there are many reminders of St.
Margaret Clitherow. Beautifully maintained and appearing as
it did in the sixteenth century is the street called The Shambles,
where the Clitherow butcher shop was located. The home of
the saint, at No. 35 The Shambles, is now a chapel in her
honor. There a service is held every Saturday. A stone memorial is located at the place of Margaret's execution, and
Catholic services are still performed in the Church of St.
Martin-le-Grand, where the saint was baptized and married.

FORTY-FIVE

BLESSED MARGARET
OF LOUVAIN

1207–1225

IN HIS *Dialogue on Miracles,* Caesarius of Heisterbach tells the story of the martyr Margaret of Louvain, who was eighteen years old at the time of her death. She was born at Louvain into humble circumstances in the year 1207. When she was old enough, she was employed as a waitress and domestic helper in the inn owned by a relative named Aubert. He was a good and pious man who frequently housed needy travelers without payment. Margaret, a virtuous girl, was pleased to help in these works of mercy. She labored hard and was a blessing to her employer, even though she had problems in the exercise of her chores. Because of the recollected and worthy manner in which she performed her work and because she was indifferent to the attentions and comments of men, she was called "the proud Margaret."

In the year 1225 Aubert and his wife decided to sell their business and enter religious life. During their last night at home, some evil men visited them under the pretext of wanting to offer the couple their best wishes for the future. The men were actually interested in the money the pious couple had received for their business—money that was to be given to the religious houses to which they were going. Soon after the arrival of the men, Aubert asked Margaret to fetch some wine for their guests. As soon as Margaret left the house, the men made their evil intentions known. When the pious couple refused to relinquish the money, the men murdered them. The ruthless thieves located the money and were about to make off with it when Margaret returned with the wine.

Because Margaret had come upon the scene and discovered what had taken place, the robbers carried her to a lonely spot near the River Dyle, where they decided to kill her. But in an attempt to spare Margaret's life, one of the men offered to release her if she would make a vow to keep silent about the crime. When Margaret steadfastly refused to cooperate, she herself was murdered. Her throat was slashed and her side was stabbed.

The virginal body of the young girl was then carelessly thrown into the river. However, a supernatural light and the sounds of angelic voices aided in its discovery. The clergy of St. Peter's Collegiate Church at Louvain claimed the body and carried it in a solemn procession to their churchyard for burial. Here miracles soon were reported.

The Cistercian monk, Caesarius, asks in his *Dialogue on Miracles*, "What would you say was the cause of martyrdom in the case of this girl?" The answer was:

> Simplicity and an innocent life. . . . There are different kinds of martyrdom, namely, innocence, as in Abel; uprightness, as in the Prophets and St. John the Baptist; love of the Law, as in the Machabees; confession of the Faith, as in the Apostles. For all these different causes Christ the Lamb is said to have been "slain from the beginning of the world."

To this Butler adds, "All Christian virtues, being protestations of our faith and proofs of our fidelity to God, are a true motive of martyrdom."

The veneration paid to the virgin martyr was approved in 1905 by Pope St. Pius X. It is said that devotion to Bl. Margaret of Louvain has been active from the time of her death in 1225 to the present.

FORTY-SIX

BLESSED MARGARET POLE

1471–1541

MARGARET Plantagenet Pole was the niece of two English kings, Edward IV and Richard III. Their brother, George Plantagenet, the duke of Clarence, was her father; her mother was Isabel, the eldest daughter of the Earl of Warwick. Henry VII, whose wife was Margaret's cousin, gave Margaret in marriage to Sir Reginald Pole, a Buckinghampshire gentleman. The marriage, contracted in 1491, produced five children; it ended after nineteen years, in 1510, with Reginald's death. Of Margaret's five children, the fourth, Reginald, was to become cardinal and archbishop of Canterbury. He was also to be the indirect cause of his mother's martyrdom.

When Henry VIII ascended the throne of England, he conferred on Margaret Pole the title of countess of Salisbury and described her as the saintliest woman in England. He also passed an Act of Restitution by which Margaret came into possession of her ancestral domains, which had been forfeited by attainder during the previous reign.

When Princess Mary was born to Henry VIII and Catherine of Aragon, the sponsor chosen for the royal infant was Margaret Pole, who was also appointed governess of the princess and head of her household. In time, Henry became attracted to Anne Boleyn, whom he wanted to marry—but first there was the matter of his marriage to Catherine. The King tried every means to have the Pope annul the marriage, but when the Pope refused to do this, that is, to grant an annulment, Henry himself declared the marriage invalid.

When the King married Anne Boleyn, Princess Mary was still in Margaret's care. However, Margaret was promptly removed from her post, even though she begged to remain and serve her royal charge.

After Anne Boleyn's fall, Margaret returned to court; but when her son Reginald wrote his treatise *Pro Ecclesiasticae Unitatis Defensione* (In Defense of the Unity of the Church), which was a work against the royal claim to ecclesiastical supremacy, and refused to return to England from his self-imposed exile, Henry VIII became so incensed that he expressed the desire to rid himself of Margaret's entire family.

In November of 1538, two of Margaret's sons and others of their family were arrested on a charge of treason and were committed to the Tower. With the exception of Geoffrey Pole, they were executed in January. Ten days after the apprehension of her sons, Margaret was also arrested and was examined by Fitzwilliam, earl of Southampton, and Goodrich, bishop of Ely. They reported to Cromwell that although they had "travailed with her" for many hours, she would "nothing utter." They concluded that either she did not share in her sons' treason, or else she was "the most arrant traitress that ever lived." Butler comments, "They had to own that the tall, dignified woman had the brains as well as the stature of a man." She was, nevertheless, taken into custody and committed to Lord Southampton's house in Cowdray Park.

Cromwell introduced a Bill of Attainder against Bl. Margaret, and from one of her coffers he produced a white silk tunic which was embroidered on the back with intricate designs. Somehow Cromwell interpreted some of the designs as representing the Five Holy Wounds. He claimed that this connected her with Sir Henry Neville's and Bl. Thomas Percy's uprising in the north and the conspiracy connected with it, since the banner of their troops had borne symbols of the holy wounds. For this false charge Parliament condemned her to death without a trial. Other charges were pressed against her, to which she was never permitted to reply.

Following her conviction, Bl. Margaret was removed to the Tower where, for nearly two years, she suffered from the cold and from insufficient clothing.

On May 28, 1541, Bl. Margaret was told that she would die within the hour. Declaring that she was not guilty of the crimes lodged against her, she nevertheless walked calmly from her cell to the East Smithfield Green, within the precincts of the Tower, where a low wooden block had been prepared for her beheading. The regular executioner being absent, his understudy performed the deed and clumsily hacked at her neck. Margaret Pole was seventy years of age. Margaret was beatified in 1886, together with other English martyrs. Remembering the kindness that Henry VIII had extended to Bl. Margaret Pole at the beginning of his reign, it is ironic that she is considered to have been the first woman martyred under his Act of Supression and his persecution of Catholics.

FORTY-SEVEN

SAINT MARGARET WARD AND BLESSED JOHN ROCHE

D. 1588

MARGARET Ward is referred to in her biographies as "Mrs. Ward," but nothing is told of her husband, family or early life. We are simply informed that she was born at Congleton, in Cheshire, of a gentleman's family and "was in the service" of a lady of distinction, Mrs. Whitall, in London.

Margaret's history actually begins with the priest, Richard Watson, a virtuous and zealous missionary, who had labored hard and successfully in the Lord's service. Under the edicts of Henry VIII, priests were considered traitors whose activities were punishable by death.

The Rev. Watson was eventually apprehended. Having suffered torture, insupportable labors, the intense miseries of his confinement and human frailty, Rev. Watson unfortunately agreed to attend a Protestant service and thereby gain his freedom. But when he was free, his conscience troubled him so much that he visited one of the prisons where his fellow priests were suffering. He confessed his sin and was absolved. To correct the bad example he had given and to relieve his conscience, he visited the same Protestant church, stood in the middle of the congregation and declared in a loud voice that he had made a mistake in attending their services, which "you untruly call the service of God, for it is indeed the service of the devil." He was immediately apprehended and dragged to prison, where he was placed in a small cell in the dungeon. For a whole month he was given only a little bread and water. He was then transferred "to a lodging at the top of the place," where his condition was made even worse by threats, harrassments and insults. The priest's sufferings were at length made known to the Catholic community, but no one dared to visit or help him for fear of being apprehended. Only Mrs. Ward had the courage to step forward.

To obtain permission to visit Rev. Watson, Margaret first became acquainted with the jailer's wife. She finally obtained permission to make occasional visits to the priest, provided that the jailers were permitted to examine her basket of provisions both before and after her visits. These examinations were meant to prevent letters from being given to the priest or sent out by means of his visitor. Gradually the guards began to trust Mrs. Ward and admitted her without examination.

Rev. Watson then devised a plan by which he could escape—provided he had a rope. Mrs. Ward obtained a rope and smuggled it in under the bread and other food in her basket. Arrangements were made for two Catholic watermen to anchor their boat near Bridewell Prison between two and three in the morning. Almost at the last moment, one of the boatmen refused to participate in the plan. Mrs. Ward confided her difficulty to her young Irish servant John Roche, alias Neale, who decided to help her.

At the appointed time, Rev. Watson, misjudging the distance between the top of the building and the ground, doubled the rope and let himself down. On reaching the end of the rope, about halfway down the building, he could do nothing else but fall the rest of the way. He did so, landing on top of a shed whose roof gave in with a loud noise. The priest was not only stunned in the fall, but also broke an arm and a leg in the process. Helped by the watermen, the priest exchanged clothes with John Roche and was making his escape when he remembered the rope. He asked one of the men to fetch it, saying that if they did not retrieve it the woman who had brought it to him would suffer for having helped him to escape. But since the noise had alerted the guards, there was no time to return for the rope. The priest made his escape, but the guards, on seeing the rope, immediately suspected that Mrs. Ward had been instrumental in providing it to the prisoner. John Roche was soon captured because the priest's clothing, which he wore, betrayed his part in the plot.

The following morning, justices and constables went to Mrs. Ward's home, rushed in, apprehended her and carried her to prison, where she was put in chains. She remained in that state for eight days. She was then hung by the hands, with her toes barely reaching the floor. She remained in this situation for so long a time that she became crippled and paralyzed. When she was brought to the court, she was asked by the judges if she "was guilty of that treachery to the Queen, and to the laws of the realm, by furnishing the means by which a traitor had escaped from justice." With a cheerful countenance Mrs. Ward answered that "she had never in her life done anything of which she less repented than the delivering of that innocent lamb from the hands of those bloody wolves." She repeatedly refused to attend the church of which Queen Elizabeth professed head, or to ask pardon of the Queen, or to do anything that was contrary to her conscience and her allegiance to the Catholic faith.

Margaret Ward was sentenced to be hanged, drawn and quartered. Challoner reports that "she was executed at Tyburn, August 30, 1588, shewing to the end a wonderful constancy and alacrity, by which the spectators were much moved and greatly edified." Bl. John Roche was also hanged, drawn and quartered at Tyburn on August 30, 1588.

As for the Rev. Watson, after his injuries were healed, he was one day walking down a street when he met his former jailer, who recognized him. After he was apprehended, he confessed the details of his escape and was subsequently martyred.

St. Margaret Ward was canonized by Pope Paul VI in 1970.

FORTY-EIGHT

VENERABLE NICHOLAS HORNER

D. 1590

DURING the reign of Queen Elizabeth, when priests were considered traitors and those who hid or aided them were liable to be severely punished, there lived in London a tailor, Nicholas Horner, who is said to have been a "good and perfect Catholic, a man of plain and just dealing."

Nicholas was apprehended for harboring priests and was imprisoned in a place of detention known as Newgate. According to their usual custom, the jailors clamped irons on both the prisoner's legs, even though one of his legs was seriously injured. The iron aggravated the condition to such an extent that amputation of the leg was inevitable. Afraid that he would give scandal to his fellow Catholics in the prison by impatience or cries of pain during the amputation, Nicholas prayed fervently to Almighty God. As Nicholas reported later, he received comfort from a certain good priest who was in prison called "Mr. Hewett," who was later martyred. This priest consoled the patient by "holding the head of Nicholas betwixt his hands whilst it was adoing (the amputation)... and by means of a certain meditation, which he purposely used at the beginning of the pain, which was of Christ bearing

His Cross to the Mount of Calvary. Of all these things many other Catholics were also eye and ear witnesses."

Pollen, in his *Acts of English Martyrs,* continues:

> But afterwards when it was cut off it pleased God to give Nicholas such patience that he not only comforted the other Catholics that were there prisoners, but also drove the surgeons and other strangers that beheld the same into admiration. For whilst it was in cutting off, he being made to sit on a form neither bound nor holden by any violence, neither offered to stir nor used any impatient screech or cries, but wringing his hands in very good order, often said, "Jesus, increase my pains and increase my patience."

Because the wound of the amputation was slow in healing, Ven. Nicholas endured almost twelve months of intense pain. Many outside the prison, on learning of his condition, petitioned for his release. When he was set at liberty, he found lodging in Smithfield, but soon thereafter was apprehended again and taken to the prison named Bridewell. There he was interrogated as to the number and names of priests who had found lodging in his home. He refused to reveal this information and was hanged by the wrists until he was almost dead.

During his next court appearance, Ven. Nicholas was condemned and sentenced to die because, as two witnesses testified, he had once made a jerkin for a priest by the name of Rev. Christopher Bales, who was martyred at a later time.

When the date for his execution was set, Nicholas told certain of his fellow prisoners of a strange sight he had witnessed one night that would comfort them, assuring them that if he knew he would live, he would most certainly keep the incident to himself. The story of this vision was told by

Nicholas to a friend, who in turn transmitted it by letter to Fr. Robert Southwell, S.J. (d. 1590). It is reported by Pollen in this manner:

> After his condemnation one night, as he was in his close room alone, saying his prayers, happening to look aside, he did see about the head of his shadow against the wall, in proportion of a half circle, a far brighter light than that of the candle, even as bright as the light of the sun; and thinking that his sight failed him, did rub his eyes and looked again, and seeing the said light to continue, took off his kercher from his head to see whether it happened of any accident thereof; but notwithstanding the light continued all one a good space after. So that at last he began to think with himself, that it was a sign given him from God to signify a crown unto him. Therefore he immediately said, "O Lord, Thy will be my will," or to that effect, and so within a while it vanished away.

Within a few days Nicholas suffered martyrdom, having a title set above his head on the gibbet. His body was afterward drawn and quartered because he had relieved and assisted the priest Christopher Bales.

Having been born at Grantley, Yorkshire, England, the date unknown, Ven. Nicholas Horner died at Smithfield on the fourth of March, 1590.

FORTY-NINE

SAINT NUNILO AND SAINT ALODIA

D. 851

THE moorish caliph, Abderrahman II, terrorized Spain in the middle of the ninth century and produced for the Church many saints who defended their faith with their lives. Among these martyrs were two sisters, Nunilo and Alodia, who lived in the city of Huesca in northeastern Spain.

The early life of the two sisters was disturbed by the death of their father, a Mohammedan, and the remarriage of their Christian mother to another Mohammedan. Since the two girls had been raised in the Christian faith, they suffered much in the exercise of their faith because of the brutality of their stepfather. After making vows of virginity, they were additionally troubled when suitors began to visit their home. To avoid these young men and to be enabled to practice their religion without the criticism and restrictions of their stepfather, they obtained permission to live in the house of a Christian aunt. Here they were free to practice their devotions and to spend all their time in prayer, except for the times when they were engaged in necessary duties.

Eventually the laws of Abderrahman were published, and countless Christians suffered as a result. The piety and faith of the two girls being well-known, it was inevitable that they were among the first who were arrested. They appeared before the cadi with Christian joy and resisted the flattery that was intended to induce them to renounce their faith. Promises and special favors were likewise rejected. When all failed, threats were made until finally they were placed in the hands of wicked women who were instructed to lead them into sin. Nunilo and Alodia were divinely enlightened and protected, and after many trials the women of sin had to admit that they could not conquer their resolution. Infuriated, the cadi ordered that they be beheaded in prison, which took place in the year 851.

FIFTY

SAINT PANTALEON

D. 305

ACCORDING to the testimony of Theodoret and other early writers, St. Pantaleon was born in Nicomedia, Turkey. His father was Eustorgius, a pagan senator; his mother, a Christian, was Eubula. When he began studying medicine, Pantaleon proved to be so intelligent and competent that he was permitted to practice his trade before the completion of his formal studies. His reputation was such that he eventually became physician to Emperor Galerius Maximian. Although raised a Christian, Pantaleon became influenced by the activities and "false wisdom" of the court and, unhappily, fell into apostasy. A zealous Christian named Hermolaos awakened Pantaleon's conscience by prudent admonitions, and brought him again to the practice of virtue.

When Diocletian's persecution began in Nicomedia, Pantaleon distributed to poor Christians the wealth he had inherited upon the death of his father. For this act of charity he was betrayed by envious fellow physicians. The Emperor, whom he had medically treated, urged him to apostatize to escape certain martyrdom, but Pantaleon refused and was arrested, together with Hermolaos and two others. After bitter suffering his companions were beheaded, but Pantaleon's ordeal lasted one day longer. He was reportedly subjected to six different attempts on his life by burning, molten lead, drowning, wild beasts, the wheel and the sword. He was finally beheaded. St. Pantaleon is one of the Fourteen Holy Helpers, since he regularly treated the poor without receiving payment.

St. Pantaleon's cultus was firmly established three hundred years after his death. His relics were diffused to many parts of Italy and France, but the greater portion of these are found in the church of Lucca, where they were officially recognized in 1715.

According to the practice prevalent in the times of the early persecutions, the blood of martyrs was collected by those who held the heroes of faith in high regard. So it was that a pious lady of Nicomedia gathered the blood of Pantaleon and kept it in her home. Apparently the blood displayed some unusual activity, since merchants of Amalfi, Italy heard of it and journeyed to Nicomedia to obtain it. The blood relic was brought to Ravella, Italy, twenty-two miles from Naples, where records of the year 1112 reveal that the blood was there in the cathedral consecrated to St. Pantaleon. The blood in its ancient flask is known to liquefy on various feast days,[1] as does the blood of St. Januarius in Naples.

A famous visitor to this relic, and an observer of the miracle, was Cardinal Newman, then a newly ordained priest, who wrote from Naples to Henry Wilberforce in August, 1846. In his letter the Cardinal wrote:

---

1. For a detailed description of the blood relic and the facts concerning its extraordinary liquefaction, consult the book *Relics* by this author.

But the most strange phenomenon is what happens at Ravello, a village or town above Amalfi. There is the blood of St. Pantaleon. It is in a vessel amid the stonework of the altar—it is not touched—but on his feast in July it liquefies. And more, there is a prohibition against those who bring portions of the True Cross into the church. A person I know, not knowing the prohibition, brought in a portion—and the priest who showed the blood suddenly said, "Who has got the Holy Cross about him?" I tell you what was told me by a grave and religious man.

The unusual aspects of the miracle have been carefully documented since 1577, although the liquefaction occurred during the centuries previous to this date. It is indeed extraordinary that this sample of the martyr's blood and its unusual activity have endured for over eighteen centuries.

Together with St. Luke and Sts. Cosmas and Damian, St. Pantaleon is regarded as the patron of physicians.

FIFTY-ONE

SAINT PERPETUA AND SAINT FELICITAS

D. 203

THE names of these two saints are united in the Canon of the Mass and in biographies because they died together on the same day, only moments apart. For this reason they also share a common feast day in the calendar of saints. The major distinction between the two is that twenty-two-year-old St. Perpetua was a woman of considerable wealth, while St. Felicitas was a slave. At the time of their arrest, Perpetua was the mother of an infant, and Felicitas was an expectant mother.

The record of the passion of St. Perpetua, St. Felicitas and their companions is one of the greatest hagiological treasures that has come down to us. In the fourth century these *Acts* were publicly read in the churches of Africa and were so highly esteemed that St. Augustine found it necessary to issue a protest against their being placed on a level with the Holy Scriptures.

It was in Carthage, in the year 203, during the persecution initiated by Emperor Severus, that five catechumens were arrested because of their faith. Among the five were our two saints. At first the prisoners seem to have been held under house arrest; but in a small diary which she kept, St. Perpetua wrote:

A few days later we were lodged in prison, and I was greatly frightened because I had never known such darkness. What a day of horror! Terrible heat, owing to the crowds! Rough treatment by the soldiers! To crown all I was tormented with anxiety for my baby. Then Tertius and Pomponius, those blessed deacons who ministered to us, paid for us to be removed for a few hours to a better part of the prison and obtain some relief. Then all went out of the prison and we were left to ourselves.

My baby was brought to me and I suckled him, for he was already faint for want of food…I suffered for many days, but I obtained leave to have my baby to remain in the prison with me and, being relieved of my trouble and anxiety for him, I at once recovered my health and my prison suddenly became a palace to me and I would rather have been there than anywhere else.

Inevitably the infant was taken from her and was given to the care of its grandfather. While suffering the loss of her child, St. Perpetua was at least comforted that, "God granted that he no longer needed the breast, and that I was not to be tormented with my milk."

In an effort to have her renounce her faith in Jesus Christ and save her life, the saint's father, who was a pagan, visited her in prison before she was to be questioned and plaintively asked her to "have pity on your child." The president, Hilarian, joined with the father and said, "Spare your father's white hairs. Spare the tender years of your child. Offer a sacrifice for the prosperity of the emperors." It would have been an easy matter for St. Perpetua to renounce her faith and to reclaim her child and the family she loved, but when asked once again, "Are you a Christian?" she readily accepted the sacrifice of separation and replied, "Yes, I am."

One of St. Perpetua's fellow Christians in prison was St. Felicitas, who had been arrested with her. As an expectant mother, Felicitas knew that a woman in her condition would not be martyred until after the child's birth. Not wanting to be separated from her companions—but wanting to die with them—she and her companions prayed that her baby would be born one month earlier than expected, otherwise Felicitas would be scheduled to die with common criminals.

The prayers of the pious souls were answered. Three days before the date set for their martyrdom, Felicitas began her labor. During her difficult delivery a jailer scoffed at her, "You are groaning now. What will you do when you are thrown to the beasts, which you did not care about when you refused to sacrifice?" Felicitas answered, "Now I myself suffer what I am suffering; but then there will be another in me who will suffer for me, because I am to suffer for Him."

Assisted by St. Perpetua, Felicitas was delivered of a healthy daughter. But soon after the baby was born, Felicitas had to part with it. She gave up the child joyfully for Jesus' sake, and committed it to the charge of her sister, a Christian, who promised to raise it with care.

When the day arrived for the martyrdom, the guards wanted to dress the men as priests of Saturn and the women as priestesses of Ceres; but the martyrs refused, saying, "We are come here of our own free will…We have sacrificed our lives to avoid doing such things. This was our agreement with you." The guards relented and permitted them to wear their regular clothes into the arena.

St. Perpetua and St. Felicitas, together with their Christian companions, first were cruelly scourged. They were stripped almost naked and were made to pass before a long line of the officers of the amphitheater, each of whom struck them with whips that were fortified with balls of lead or iron. When the martyrs reached the end of the line their bodies were torn and bleeding. Afterward they were brought before the crowd to be killed by wild beasts.

Clothed in light garments, Sts. Perpetua and Felicitas were presented to a mad heifer, which tossed St. Perpetua first. She fell on her side, but she soon came to herself—and seeing that her dress was torn, she modestly arranged the garment and adjusted her hair. Upon noticing that St. Felicitas had also been tossed by the animal and was lying bruised, St. Perpetua helped her up. The spectators, now feeling pity for the two women, would not allow them again to be exposed to the animal. The two were accordingly led away to the gate called the *Sana Vivaria*. On seeing her brother along the way, as well as Rusticus, a catechuman who was a great friend of hers, St. Perpetua told them, "Stand firm in the Faith, love one another, and do not be frightened at our sufferings."

Those who survived the attacks of wild animals in the amphitheater were generally dispatched by the sword. After she gave Perpetua the kiss of peace, St. Felicitas stepped forward first, suffered the blow and expired in silence. St. Perpetua happened to fall victim to an unskilled executioner, who wounded her in the neck without killing her. She at first cried out in pain, but then recovered and calmly guided the man's trembling hand. She received the fatal thrust of the blade and expired.

SAINT PERPETUA AND SAINT FELICITAS

The martyrdom of St. Perpetua and St. Felicitas took place in the year 203, on the seventh of March—the day on which the Church continues to celebrate their feast day.

FIFTY-TWO

SAINT PHILEMON AND SAINT APOLLONIUS

D. 305

DURING the persecution of Diocletian, it was the obligation of each citizen to honor the gods by offering sacrifice to them. Realizing that refusal to do this would result in their imprisonment and possible death, many frightened Christians occasionally hired pagans to offer this sacrifice in their stead. Certificates stating that they had complied with their obligation were to be brought back to them by the pagans who had taken their places. According to Butler, the Church did not necessarily regard these Christians as apostates and merely compelled these *libellatici* to do penance for this cowardly act.

Apollonius was well aware of the sufferings endured by many Christians who refused to deny their faith by sacrificing to the false gods. To avoid a similar end, he planned to escape detection as a Christian by hiring someone to take his place at a pagan ceremony. A well-known piper and dancer named Philemon was willing to do this favor for the price of four gold coins. To prepare himself, Philemon asked that he be given some of Apollonius' clothes and a cape with a hood so that he could conceal his face. While disguised in this manner, he went before the judge for questioning and to perform the rite. But when it came time to offer sacrifice, Philemon was suddenly converted by the Holy Spirit. He declared his belief in Jesus Christ and refused to acknowledge the idols.

When Philemon's true identity was made known, all who were present accepted the incident as a jest, thinking that the piper-dancer was also capable of impersonations. When the laughter was over and Philemon was asked in all serious-ness to comply with the Emperor's edicts, the saint, who had received baptism by desire, stoutly refused to do so.

Apollonius was arrested during this time. Ashamed of his cowardice, he courageously proclaimed his belief in Jesus Christ, and to make amends for his weakness he per-sistently refused to recant, although there existed the possi-bility of torture.

The two saints were eventually martyred in the year 305 by being sewn up in sacks and cast into the sea.

FIFTY-THREE

BLESSED PIERINA MOROSINI

1931–1957

THE family of Rocco and Sara Morosini included nine sons and Pierina, who was the only daughter and the oldest of the children. Born on January 7, 1931, Pierina lived a peaceful and prayerful life with her family on a small farm in Fiobbio, which is located in the Diocese of Bergamo in northern Italy.

Always a pious child, Pierina received the sacraments according to the custom of the time. She was quick of mind and proved to be a willing assistant to her mother by helping with her brothers and performing chores, both inside the house and outside in the fields.

After finishing elementary school, Pierina enrolled in a sewing class and learned how to make clothes for the entire family. In addition to all the help she gave her family, Pierina wanted to assist them financially, and for this reason, when she was only fifteen years old, she began working at a cotton mill in nearby Albino.

Separating the small town of Fiobbio and Albino was a hilly, forested area through which Pierina had to walk twice a day. She always recited her morning prayers on the path, received Holy Communion in the Church of Albino and then began her work at six in the morning with the Sign of the Cross. Her co-workers remember her as being cheerful, but not very talkative. They also claimed that she seemed to work while in a profound union with God.

After returning from a hard day's work, Pierina helped with the chores of the household. She was also an active member of an organization for young people known as Catholic Action. At the age of sixteen, she was named parish director of members in her age group. Pierina also distinguished herself among her townspeople by her devoted work on behalf of missionaries and the diocesan seminary. She also assisted in the cleaning of the church and endeared herself to all because of her sweet disposition and humble demeanor. Her many works of charity are said to be the result of her deep prayer life, which was woven throughout the various parts of her day.

Pierina had a profound attraction to the religious life and wanted to do missionary work among the lepers. Her aunt, who was a nun, recalls that when Pierina was a child she told her aunt in all confidence, "I want to be a nun and belong to Jesus."

Since the needs of her family prevented Pierina from leaving, she accepted the family's decision as being the will of God and never spoke of her great disappointment. Realizing that Pierina might never be able to join the religious life, her spiritual director permitted her to make private vows of chastity, poverty and obedience. To help herself maintain these vows as perfectly as possible, she wrote a twelve-point rule, which she observed for the rest of her life. In addition, she joined the Apostolate of Reparation, offering in a spirit of faith the many difficulties she encountered each day.

Pierina spent all of her life in Fiobbio and Albino, and never left except for a trip she made to Rome with members of Catholic Action. This took place in April, 1947, for the beatification of Maria Goretti, the little saint who had died in the defense of purity. During the journey, the life of Maria Goretti understandably was the frequent topic of conversation. When Pierina was asked what she would do if she were confronted by an assailant, Pierina quickly replied that she would willingly imitate Maria Goretti by dying in the defense of purity. On another occasion she again stated that she would rather die than commit a sin.

Sometime after this trip to Rome, Pierina seems to have had a premonition that she would suffer martyrdom. Ten years later, this premonition was realized. On April 4, 1957, while she was on her way home from work, Pierina was confronted on the wooded path by a young man. Judging from the condition in which she was found and the many bloodied handprints in the area, Pierina had fought vigorously against the rapist and even attempted to crawl away. Found in the weeds nearby was a rock that was covered with blood and bits of flesh. This rock was in the shape of a hammer, and it was apparent that the man had used it to repeatedly strike Pierina in the head.

One of Pierina's brothers reported that on the day of Pierina's assault, he had a premonition that something would happen to her and was very agitated concerning her welfare. It was for this reason that he went along the wooded path to meet her after her work shift to accompany her home.

Instead, he found his dying sister on the ground with her clothes in disarray and her long hair matted with blood. When her brother drew nearer, Pierina slowly moved her hand to her head, but did not speak or open her eyes. He reported that her face was bloody and her breathing was slow and labored. When he touched the left side of her face, which was covered by her hair, his hand was immediately covered with blood and pieces of flesh. It was obvious that a huge and ugly wound covered the left side of her face and head. The brother ran for help and returned with various relatives, who were shocked by what they discovered. It was then noted that the assailant had neatly arranged beside his victim her shoes, socks, purse, rosary and a photograph taken of her with three of her friends.

Pierina was removed to a hospital, where she was treated for her injuries; but she lapsed into a deep coma and died two days later, before she could describe or identify her assailant. Pierina was twenty-six years old. Her doctors reported that she was a victim of sexual aggression, to which one of the doctors added, "We have here a new Maria Goretti." The Vatican newspaper *L'Osservatore Romano* (October 5, 1987) reported that, "Her skull was broken and she was raped." Pierina is nevertheless designated as "virgin" as well as "martyr."

The funeral of the virtuous Pierina was attended by most of the people of Fiobbio and Albino. The crime committed against her so outraged the people that it quickly became well-known throughout the district. For this reason an article on the front page of the newspaper of Bergamo told of her life and death and was accompanied by a picture of the huge crowd that attended the funeral.

A memorial marker and a stone which recorded the heroism of Pierina were soon erected at the wooded place where she had been found mortally wounded. A larger memorial stone, which is topped with a marble bust resembling Pierina, is found in the piazza of the Church of Fiobbio.

During the ecclesiastical examination into the life of Pierina conducted in preparation for her beatification, the casket containing her remains was removed from her tomb on April 9, 1983. It was then carried in an impressive procession to the parish church of Fiobbio, where her relics are now entombed. This shrine attracts many of her devotees, who pray fervently for her intercession. It is customary for many to walk in procession to the place of martyrdom.

Pierina Morosini was beatified on October 4, 1987. Sara Morosini, Pierina's mother, had already met Pope John Paul II in 1981, but was privileged to meet him once again shortly after the beatification ceremony, while he was still seated upon the papal throne. While Sara Morosini knelt before him, the Pope placed his hands upon her head and spoke words of comfort. After the ceremony, the Pope again spoke privately with her and then met with Pierina's brothers and other members of the family.

Kept as a treasured relic is Pierina's copy of a biography of St. Maria Goretti. It is said that this book was Pierina's favorite and that she read it so often, she almost knew it from memory.

Pierina has been recommended as a model for working girls and as a model for holy purity.

FIFTY-FOUR

SAINT POLLIO

D. 304

BUTLER tells us that "there can be no doubt about the historical existence of St. Pollio," who served as lector in the ancient episcopal city of Cibales.

After the martyrdom of Bishop Eusebius, Pollio became the leader of those Christians in the diocese who remained true to the Faith and ignored the edicts of Diocletian.

Finally brought before Governor Probus, St. Pollio boldly confessed that he was not only a Christian, but he was also the chief of all the lectors in the city. When Probus asked, "Of what lectors?" Pollio answered, "Of those who read the Word of God to the people." When Pollio refused to sacrifice to the gods, Probus ordered the decapitation of the saint. But when Pollio responded that he would be happy to suffer for Jesus Christ, Probus became so enraged that he changed his order from the swift death of decapitation to that of having Pollio burned alive.

When Pollio was led to the place of execution, he offered himself as a sacrifice to God and suffered courageously on the twenty-eighth of April, in the year 304.

FIFTY-FIVE

SAINT POLYEUCTUS

FOURTH CENTURY

ST. POLYEUCTUS was a wealthy Roman officer of Greek parentage. While still a pagan he made friends with a Christian named Nearchus, who eventually converted him to the Faith. When news of the persecution ordered by the Emperor reached Armenia, where Polyeuctus lived, he prepared to affirm his faith, should he be asked concerning it. Polyeuctus bravely announced his Christianity when the time came and declared that he was eager to die for the Faith. He was promptly apprehended and condemned to cruel tortures. After the executioners grew weary of tormenting him, they tried to persuade him with arguments to renounce his faith.

As if imprisonment, torture and arguing were not enough to discourage the saint, his wife, Pauline, his children and his father-in-law visited him in prison and by means of tears and entreaties tried to convince him to renounce Christianity and return home with them. But the saint withstood this heart-rending offer and became more resolute in his faith. He steadfastly continued his profession of faith in Jesus Christ, and, as a result, he was condemned to death.

On the road to the place of execution, Polyeuctus exhorted the bystanders to renounce their idols and spoke

213

so convincingly that many were converted. After he was beheaded, the Christians buried his body in the city.

Nearchus, who had converted him, gathered the saint's blood in a cloth, and later wrote his *Acts*.

A church is known to have been dedicated to St. Polyeuctus before the year 377 at Melitene in Armenia. As a Roman officer, Polyeuctus had been stationed in this city with his troops. It is also the city where the saint suffered and died.

FIFTY-SIX

SAINT POTAMIANA

D. 202

ST. POTAMIANA was a young, pious and extremely beautiful slave whose master offered to free her at the expense of her chastity. Eventually, her steadfast refusals made him realize that he would probably never win her consent. Determined to try another tactic, he applied to the Prefect of Egypt, promising him a large sum of money if he could persuade the virgin to yield to him. If Potamiana still refused, the Prefect was asked to put her to death as a Christian.

The Prefect summoned Potamiana and showed her all the instruments of torture and used all his wiles to induce her to obey her master. At his constant urgings, the saint at last replied, "How is it possible that there can be found a judge so unjust as to condemn me because I will not satisfy the inordinate desires of a lewd person?" When the saint remained firm, she was condemned to be stripped and cast into a cauldron of boiling pitch.

Upon hearing the sentence, Potamiana said to the judge, "I beg of you, by the life of the Emperor whom you honor, not to oblige me to appear unclothed; rather suffer me to be slowly lowered into the cauldron fully dressed that you may see the patience which Jesus Christ, whom you know not, bestows upon those who trust Him."

The Prefect granted her request. A guard named Basilides, who was charged with leading her to the place of execution, treated the slave with the utmost respect and protected her from the insults and pressure of the crowd. Potamiana thanked him for his courtesy and told him that after her death she would pray to God for his salvation.

Upon reaching the place of martyrdom, Potamiana was lowered feet first into the cauldron of boiling pitch until the liquid covered her head. Her pious mother, Marcella, was martyred at the same time, in the year 202.

After witnessing the modesty and courage of Potamiana, Basilides surprised his fellow soldiers by refusing to take an oath when called upon to do so. He acknowledged himself a Christian and was consigned to prison. To fellow prisoners he revealed that Potamiana had appeared to him the third or fourth night after her martyrdom and had placed on his head a crown which she said she had won for him by her prayers. He received baptism in prison, and after professing his faith, he was beheaded.

FIFTY-SEVEN

BLESSED RALPH MILNER

D. 1591

A S A husband and the father of seven children, Ralph Milner supported his family by farming near the city of Winchester, England. He was entirely illiterate and was raised as a Protestant who looked upon the sovereign of his country as the head of the Church of England. After observing the lives of the Catholics with whom he was acquainted and seeing how many of them refused to deny their faith, even though the denial would result in a heroic death, he was greatly inspired. He was eventually instructed in the Faith and was baptized, but on the very day of his First Holy Communion he was arrested for his beliefs. He was kept a prisoner for a number of years and was often released on parole. Since his guards trusted him, he was able to take advantage of his friendship with them to aid his fellow prisoners and to smuggle priests into the prison to administer the sacraments to those who were closely confined.

Ralph Milner did not focus his activities only on relieving prisoners. Because of his knowledge of the countryside, he often guided missionary priests to areas where Catholics were in need of spiritual guidance. In this activity he became acquainted with Father Stanney, S.J., who afterward wrote

the saint's biography. According to Challoner, Father Stanney
took notice that

> Ralph Milner used to come once a month to the house where
> this priest resided, to conduct him about the villages, there to
> preach and administer the Sacraments to the poor; who also
> declares in his preface that he can testify that, ignorant as he
> [Ralph] was, he had, by the bright light of his virtues and by
> his fervent prayers, been, under God, the cause of the conver-
> sion of many to the Catholic Faith.

When Bl. Ralph broadened the areas of his activities, a
secular priest, Fr. Roger Dickenson, came from Lincoln to
assist Fr. Stanney. Fr. Dickenson was soon arrested, but was
able to escape when his guards became intoxicated. The second time he was apprehended, both he and Ralph Milner
were brought to trial: Fr. Dickenson for being a priest, Ralph
Milner for assisting him.

At the trial, the judge had pity on Bl. Ralph, who was
advanced in age and was the father of a large family. Seeking
a pretext to set him free, the judge said that if Ralph Milner
would consent to say his prayers in the nearby Protestant
church, it would be taken as a gesture of his reconciliation
with the Church of England and he would be free to live the
rest of his years in peace. But since this act would serve as a
renunciation of his Catholic faith, Bl. Ralph refused to do so.
Challoner relates that Bl. Ralph answered, "Would your lordship then advise me, for the perishable trifles of this world,
or for a wife and children, to lose my God? No, my Lord, I
cannot approve or embrace a counsel so disagreeable to the
maxims of the Gospel."

Challoner relates that his friends and ministers tried every argument to entice him to renounce his faith and thereby win his release.

> Even when he was at the very gallows, they ceased not to tempt him; and sent his seven children to him, to move him to relent by the sight of them; but his heart was too strongly fixed on God to be overcome by flesh and blood. He gave them, therefore, his last blessing, declaring aloud that he could wish them no greater happiness, than to die for the like cause for which he was going to die.

Both he and Fr. Roger Dickenson were executed at Winchester on July 7, 1591.

FIFTY-EIGHT

SAINT REGINA

D. 251

ACCORDING to a French biography, Regina was the daughter of Clemens, a pagan citizen of Alise, in Burgundy. Since her mother died during her delivery, Regina was entrusted to the care of a Christian woman who baptized her and taught her the doctrines of the Faith.

Inspired by her love for Christ, Regina made a vow of chastity, promising that her affections would be reserved for God alone. When the time came for Regina to be returned to her father, he refused to receive her and drove her from his home after learning of her dedication to Christianity. After Regina returned to the woman who had cared for her during her youth, she found it necessary to support herself by tending sheep.

One day while the fifteen-year-old Regina was tending her flocks, she attracted the attention of Olybrius, the prefect of Gaul. He expressed the desire to marry her, but Regina refused his proposal; nor would she listen to the attempted persuasions of her father, who was willing to accept her now that there was the prospect of a distinguished marriage.

Despite her refusal, Olybrius sent for her, and as she again rejected his proposal he became furious and had her placed in a dungeon. When she remained constant in her vow of virginity, Olybrius ordered her to be tortured. One account states that she was whipped and was then tortured with hot plates and burning pincers, as well as with iron combs. During her torment she continually praised God until finally Olybrius found it necessary to silence her by cutting her throat.

The relics of St. Regina were translated in the year 864 to the Abbey of Flavigny. A portion of her relics are still venerated at Alise-Sainte-Reine, where she suffered. In comparatively recent times, the foundation of an ancient basilica which had been dedicated in her honor was found at Alise.

FIFTY-NINE

SAINT RICHARD GWYN

(ST. RICHARD WHITE)

1537–1584

THE first Welshman to suffer in his own land as the result of the persecution of Catholics by Queen Elizabeth I was St. Richard Gwyn, a schoolmaster. He was born at Llanidloes in the County of Montgomery, about the year 1537. Little else is known of his life before the time that Queen Elizabeth ascended the throne.

Gwyn completed his studies at St. John's College at Cambridge, England, where he acquired a considerable reputation as a scholar. When his friend and patron, George Bullock, master of the college, had to resign his fellowship and all academic honors for the sake of his conscience, Gwyn returned to his native North Wales and began to teach school at various places in Flintshire and Denbighshire. An old account tells that "his moderation and temperance were such that his enemies to this day could never charge him with any fault other than the following of his faith and conscience—which nowadays is accounted madness." He eventually married a virtuous lady named Catherine and became the father of six children, three of whom survived him.

Being a Catholic gentleman, he committed an error too

common in those days, that while a Catholic at heart and in principle, he nevertheless outwardly conformed to the Protestant faith and attended their services. When missionaries from Douai, France arrived in Wales to reconcile people who, like Richard, had weakened their consciences, Richard was persuaded by them to confess his mistake and to courageously profess and practice the Catholic faith. Queen Elizabeth and her ministers, on learning about the missionaries' successes, resolved to overcome their work by means of persecution. The first victim of this campaign was Richard Gwyn.

Because Richard had excused himself from the Protestant services on many occasions, his absences became so well-known that he took his family and left the area and successfully conducted schools in several other places. But in 1579, he was recognized in Wrexham by a vicar who had apostatized. Gwyn was denounced by the vicar, arrested and imprisoned in Ruthin jail, from which he later managed to escape.

In June of 1580, the Privy Council directed the Protestant bishops to be more vigilant in their dealings with Catholic recusants. The following month, Richard Gwyn was seized and brought before a magistrate, who sent him to Wrexham jail. During a court appearance he was offered his liberty if he would conform. Upon his refusal he was returned to jail, where he was secured with chains until the next session of the court.

The following May, when court was held at Wrexham, Judge Bromley was informed of Gwyn's previous participation in Protestant services and his present refusal to do so again. The judge then ordered that since Mr. Gwyn still refused to attend services, he should be taken there forcibly. Putting up as much resistance as he could, Gwyn loudly protested the violence done to him. And in the church itself, he rattled his chains and made such a disturbance that neither he, nor anyone else, could hear the minister. When Gwyn could not be silenced, the judge ordered that he be carried out and set in the stocks of the marketplace. In the meantime, an indictment was drawn up against him for having "insolently and impiously" interrupted the minister and the people in the divine worship. After a jury was impanelled, Mr. Gwyn was brought into the courtroom. When the clerk of the court began the indictment, his eyes weakened so that he could not continue reading. When the judge asked the clerk about his difficulty, he replied that he did not know, but that he could not see properly. The judge sneered, saying, "Take care lest the papists make a miracle of this."

The schoolmaster was returned to prison and was joined a short time later by two gentlemen, Mr. John Pugh and Mr. Robert Morris, who were also accused of failing to attend Protestant services. All three were arraigned for high treason and were sent from Wrexham jail to the Council of the Marches. Later in the year they suffered at Bewdley and Bridgenorth, where their jailers attempted to make them confess by whom they had been reconciled to the Catholic Church. Richard Gwyn and John Pugh courageously withstood their torments; Robert Morris weakened for a short time, but afterwards repented.

On October 11, 1584, the three men were brought to trial and indicted for high treason. Witnesses against them swore that the prisoners had said, in their hearing, that the Queen was not the head of the Church, but rather, the Pope was, and that the accused, Richard Gwyn, had attempted to reconcile Lewis Gronow to the Church of Rome. Gwyn denied any knowledge of Gronow and objected to the testimony, saying that the witnesses perjured themselves. No credence was given his claim, however.

As a last attempt to shake Richard Gwyn's resistance, the prosecutors brought into the courtroom Catherine Gwyn, who was carrying her youngest child in her arms. As the contemporary account of the trial tells, she surprised the court by declaring to the judge, "If you lack blood, you may take my life as well as my husband's; and if you will give the witnesses another bribe, they will bear evidence against me as well as they did against him." Infuriated at her remarks, the judge lost no time in instructing the jury. The twelve men deliberated and found Richard Gwyn and John Pugh guilty, but acquitted Robert Morris, who, to the surprise of the court, wept bitterly at being unable to suffer with his companions for so good a cause. Because of his behavior he was returned to prison, where he is believed to have died.

Later, one of the witnesses who had testified in court against the three prisoners made a public declaration that his evidence and that of the other two witnesses had been false, and that he had been paid by the Vicar of Wrexham and another person. John Pugh was reprieved, but Richard Gwyn suffered according to the sentence. He was hanged, cut down while still living, and his abdomen was opened. It is reported that while the hangman had his hands in the victim's bowels to remove them according to the sentence, the martyr, in his agony, was twice heard to pray, "Jesus, have mercy on me!"

He was then beheaded and his body cut into quarters.

Having been imprisoned for four years, the martyr was executed at Wrexham, in Denbighshire, on October 17, 1584. His head and one of his quarters were set upon Denbigh Castle.

During his imprisonment, Gwyn wrote a number of religious poems and a funeral ode in the Welsh language, all of which called on his countrymen to preserve the Catholic faith. Richard Gwyn was beatified in 1929 and canonized by Pope Paul VI in 1970 with thirty-nine other martyrs of England who died between the years 1535 and 1679. He is considered to be the protomartyr of Wales.

SIXTY

BLESSED RICHARD HERST

D. 1628

THE history of Bl. Richard Herst is said to be one of
the most remarkable and unusual in the annals of the
English and Welsh martyrs, since he was hanged after being
falsely charged with willful murder.

He was born near Preston, in Lancashire, and was a
successful and well-to-do farmer. But because Bl. Richard
would not conform to the Anglican Church, of which Queen
Elizabeth had claimed supremacy, the authorities called for
his arrest. Sent to apprehend him was Christopher Norcross,
who engaged the help of two men, Wilkinson and Dewhurst.

They found Bl. Richard plowing a field, and as Norcross
handed him the warrant, Wilkinson struck at the humble
farmer with a staff. A girl who was working in another part of
the field, seeing this unwarranted attack, ran to summon her
mistress, who came running out with a farmhand and another
man by the name of Bullen, who was visiting at the time.

The process servers turned to meet the farmhand and the
visitor and knocked them down. At almost the same time, the
girl hit Dewhurst over the head. The process servers then ran
away, but as Challoner relates, Dewhurst "partly on occasion
of the blow, partly also to apply himself close to Wilkinson,

made more haste than good speed, and ran so disorderly over the hard-ploughed lands as that he fell down and broke his leg." The fracture became infected, and thirteen days later Dewhurst died of gangrene, after having declared that his fall had been quite accidental.

Despite this deathbed declaration, Richard Herst was indicted for murder before Sir Henry Yelverton. During the trial, it was declared by two witnesses that Dewhurst's fall had been an accident, and that at the time the maid gave Dewhurst the blow upon the head, Richard Herst was at least thirty yards away and had not given the girl any direction or encouragement to do such a thing. The jury who heard the few facts of the case delivered a verdict of not guilty. However, the judge was not satisfied with the verdict. Speaking privately with the foreman, he persuaded him to deliberate again and to bring back a verdict of guilty, since he felt that the defendant should be convicted "as an example."

Since the first charge brought against Richard Herst had been that he was a nonconformist, Bl. Richard's freedom was offered him if he would take the Oath of Supremacy, which had been condemned by the Holy See. Richard Herst refused to do so. A guilty verdict was promptly rendered, and a sentence of death was declared as punishment.

The day before he suffered, Bl. Richard was ordered to attend a service in a Protestant church. Since Richard refused to go, the High Sheriff ordered him to be dragged by force. While Richard Herst offered all the resistance he could, he was dragged over ragged and stony ground to the church. When he arrived he "cast himself upon the ground and thrust his fingers into his ears that he might not hear their doctrine."

On returning to prison, he happily told all the Catholics along the way, "They have tortured my body, but I thank God they have not hurt my soul."

During the time of his confinement, Richard Herst wrote three letters to his confessor. In one of these letters, all of which are still preserved, Bl. Richard wrote,

> Although my flesh be timorous and fearful, I yet find great comfort in spirit in casting myself upon my sweet Saviour with a most fervent love, when I consider what He hath done and suffered for me, and my greatest desire is to suffer with Him. And I had rather choose to die a thousand deaths than to possess a kingdom and live in mortal sin; for there is nothing so hateful to me as sin, and that only for the love of my Saviour.

In another letter to his confessor he wrote, "I pray you remember my poor children." Richard Herst had six young children at the time, and one yet unborn.

Before leaving his cell on the day of his execution, he looked toward the castle and saw hanging there the head of the priest, Bl. Edmund Arrowsmith, who had died the day before. On being asked at what he was looking, Richard Herst answered, "I look at the head of that blessed martyr whom you have sent before to prepare the way for us."

As he was traveling to the place of execution, Bl. Richard was met in the street by Mr. King, the vicar of the town, who questioned him about his faith. Richard Herst answered, "I believe according to the faith of the Holy Catholic Church." Bl. Richard carried with him a picture of Christ crucified on which he looked frequently, repeating short ejaculatory prayers as he did so. On reaching the scaffold, he paused to say a final prayer, but on seeing that the hangman was fumbling while trying to adjust the rope, Richard Herst called up to him, "Tom, I think I must come up and help thee."

Richard Herst died on August 29, 1628 and was beatified in 1929.

SIXTY-ONE

SAINT SABAS

D. 372

WHEN Athanaric, a king of the Goths, raised a persecution against his Christian subjects, many Goths who had converted to Christianity were martyred. Of the fifty-one Gothic martyrs commemorated by the Greeks, the most famous is St. Sabas, who served as lector to the priest Sansala.

At the beginning of the persecution, the magistrates ordered that all Christians should offer a token sacrifice to the gods by eating meat that previously had been consecrated to the idols. Some pagans who had Christian relatives and friends whom they wished to save, persuaded certain officials to give these Christians meat that had not been offered to the gods.

St. Sabas spoke loudly against this hypocrisy. He refused to eat the meat himself and declared that those who did accept and eat the unconsecrated meat under these conditions were betrayers of the Faith. While a few Christians agreed with him, the greater part of the Christian community was so displeased with his opinion that they forced him to leave the city.

A year after St. Sabas was permitted to return, another persecution began. The Christian leaders of the town, still fearful of what would happen to them if they acknowledged their Christianity, offered to swear to the persecutors that there were no Christians in the town. St. Sabas could have left or kept quiet, but instead he waited until the oath was about to take place. Bravely presenting himself to the authorities he said, "Let no one swear for me; I am a Christian!" When the authorities learned that he had no worldly possessions except the clothes he wore, he was released with the remark: "Such a fellow can do us neither good nor harm."

A few years later, when the persecution again threatened the lives of Christians, soldiers broke into the lodging of the priest Sansala, with whom Sabas was staying. The priest was surprised in his sleep and was bound and thrown into a cart. Sabas was pulled from his pallet and was dragged through thorn bushes and whipped with sticks. Because the persecutors were determined to make him suffer still more, a rack was fashioned from the "axle-trees" of a cart. With his outstretched hands and feet bound to it, St. Sabas was tortured for a considerable part of the night. When his torturers finally decided to rest, a compassionate woman unfastened the saint, but he refused to escape.

The next day, St. Sabas was suspended from the beam of a house. Later both Sabas and the priest were offered meat that had been offered to idols. When both men stoutly refused to touch it, Sabas was struck in the chest with a javelin. Since this did not kill him, orders were given that he should be drowned.

St. Sabas was subsequently taken to the banks of the Mussovo River, where his head was held under the water with a plank until he expired. According to a letter written on behalf of the local Christians to the church in Cappadocia very shortly after the martyrdom, St. Sabas' death appears to have taken place on April 12, 372, at the place now called Targoviste, northwest of Bucharest in Romania.

The saint's body was drawn from the water and left on the shore, but it was recovered by the faithful and was sent by Junius Soranus, the Christian duke of Scythia, to the saint's country of Caesarea in Cappadocia, where St. Basil welcomed it.

SIXTY-TWO

SAINT SERENUS

D. C. 307

KNOWN as "The Gardener," St. Serenus was a Greek by birth who left all that he had to serve God in the ascetical life of celibacy, penance and prayer.

Upon reaching the area now known as Yugoslavia, he bought a garden, which he cultivated. Surrounded by the beauty and peace of the countryside, his body was nourished by the fruit and vegetables his garden produced while his soul benefited from his constant prayers and meditation.

During a persecution against the Christians, Serenus left his garden for a few months until peace was again established. Then one day after his return, he found a woman walking in the garden during the early afternoon, at an hour when people of stature were usually resting. When he courteously reminded her that it seemed an improper time for a woman of her position to be walking alone in the garden of an ascetic, the woman became insulted and furious. She immediately wrote to her husband, who belonged to the guards of the Emperor Maximian, and complained that she had been grievously offended by Serenus.

After receiving the letter, the woman's husband went to the Emperor to demand justice for his wife, who had been insulted in a distant land. He was given a letter addressed to the Governor of the province which would enable him to obtain satisfaction. In due time, Serenus was brought before the Governor to reply to the charge made against his conduct.

In answer to the Governor's questions, Serenus acknowledged that he was a gardener and that he had never insulted a woman in his whole life. He remembered that a woman of stature had been found walking in his garden and that he had reminded the lady that it was an unseemly hour for a woman of position to be walking in the garden of an unmarried man.

Serenus answered the charge so sincerely that the woman's husband saw the situation from another point of view and asked that the charge of misconduct be dropped. But the Governor's suspicions were aroused in another area of the saint's conduct.

Considering that Serenus was scrupulous in his dealings with the woman, he suspected that Serenus was a Christian and proceeded to question him. The saint readily acknowledged that he was a Christian and that he was willing to suffer for the Faith. Without further questioning, St. Serenus was condemned to suffer death by decapitation. His martyrdom occurred about the year 307.

SIXTY-THREE

SAINT SIMON OF TRENT

D. 1475

IN THE Office for the feast of the Holy Innocents we read, "These children cry out their praises to the Lord; by their death they have proclaimed what they could not preach with their infant voices." St. Simon of Trent (Italy) likewise cries out his praises to the Lord, having also died in his innocence at the hands of unbelievers.

Simon of Trent was two and a half years old when he was kidnapped by non-believers who wanted to express their hatred for the Church by killing a Christian child.

One of the kidnappers, a man named Tobias, found Simon playing outside his home with no one guarding him. Simon was enticed away with kindness and was brought to the home of his abductor.

During the early hours of Good Friday, in the year 1475, the child's martyrdom began. His mouth was gagged, and he was held by the arms in the form of a cross. While in this position his tender body was pierced with awls and bodkins in blasphemous mockery of the sufferings of Jesus Christ. After an hour's torture, the child died. The body was kept for a short time before it was thrown into a canal. When the body was recovered, an investigation led to the arrest of suspects.

After confessing their part in the crime, the child's murderers were severely punished.

The remains of little Simon were buried in St. Peter's Church at Trent, where many miracles took place. Simon was awarded the title of saint because of his tender age and the manner of his death.

SIXTY-FOUR

SAINT SOLANGIA

D. 880

B ORN at Villemont, France, St. Solangia (Solange) was the
child of pious parents who were vine-dressers. Although
living in poor circumstances, she was blessed with some of
heaven's most beguiling gifts. She was sweet-tempered, lov-
able, charitable, industrious and extremely beautiful.

Reports of her beauty reached Bernard de la Gothie, the
son of the Count of Poitiers. Bernard journeyed to meet
Solangia and found her in the pasture, where she was minding
her father's sheep. He immediately developed a great desire to
have her for his wife and proposed marriage.

Solangia declined the offer, giving as her excuse the vow
of virginity she had made at the age of seven. The nobleman
expressed his disappointment and pleaded with her, describ-
ing the many benefits she was renouncing for herself and her
poor family.

When Solangia continued to decline his proposal,
Bernard decided to abduct her. Bernard caught her up and set
her in the saddle before him, but Solangia resisted with such
violence that she threw herself from his horse while it was
crossing a stream. Injured in the fall, she struggled to crawl
to safety. The pride of the young nobleman was seriously

wounded. Angry at seeing the girl attempting to escape him and furious at the rejection, he decapitated her with a blow from his sword. The year was 880.

The veneration paid to St. Solangia has remained active at the Church of St. Martin at Villemont, where the head of the saint is reverently enshrined. Near her home, a field where she liked to pray received the name of Le Champ de Sainte Solangia.

In the past, during times of great calamity, the relics of the saint have been taken in procession through the town of Bourges. Although the processions no longer take place, the saint is still invoked in times of drought.

SIXTY-FIVE

SAINT SWITHIN WELLS

1536-1591

A S THE sixth son of Thomas Wells of Brambridge, England, Swithin was educated from his infancy in the ways of virtue. In his youth he engaged in innocent diversions, including hawking and hunting, yet he was always devout in prayer and dedicated to the True Faith. He is described as having been good-natured, courteous, generous, courageous, amiable and pleasant in conversation.

After he was instructed in the liberal sciences, Swithin traveled to Rome, partly to learn the Italian language and also to visit the holy places. After returning to England he was employed in noble houses, and for six years he gave himself "to a more profitable employment of training young gentlemen in virtue and learning," that is, he was a teacher in a boys' school at Monkton Farleigh in Wiltshire.

St. Swithin eventually married a good and pious woman, with whom he lived in an edifying manner. The couple had only one child, a daughter, Margaret.

Swithin moved to London in 1585 with his little family and there, for the next six years, he aided and hid priests. This was during the unfortunate time in British history when Queen Elizabeth was persecuting those who refused to acknowledge her as the head of the Church of England.

Swithin Wells always gave a good example to his neighbors and was very successful in bringing heretics and schismatics to the Catholic faith. He cautioned them not to indulge in worldly pleasures to such an extent that they would thereby neglect their prayers and devotions. He also encouraged them not to be fearful of professing their faith, but rather to despise all worldly things and, like him, to be continually advancing toward heaven. He himself practiced what he instructed others to do. He professed his faith by permitting his home to be a harbor for priests, who came at all hours of the day. Such visits by the clergy were considered an act of treason, to be punished by death. He is also known to have arranged lodging for priests where they could engage in catechetical instruction. Mr. Wells' activities became so well-known to the justices and other officials that it eventually became unsafe for anyone to be seen in his company.

In the last years of his life, Swithin Wells rented a house in Holborn, near Gray's Inn Fields, where he continued to provide assistance to a number of priests until the morning of November 8, 1591. On that day the Rev. Edmund Genings, who was a young priest, was celebrating Holy Mass in the home of Swithin and his wife, with a small group of people in attendance. In accordance with the October 18, 1591 royal proclamation which led to the stricter enforcement of the laws against Catholics in England, the celebrated priest-catcher, Topcliffe, arrived at the house with his officers. He arrested everyone in the house, including Mrs. Wells. Although Swithin Wells was not present at the time, he was arrested sometime later.

At the ensuing trial, the Rev. Edmund Genings was found guilty of being a priest, Swithin Wells of harboring priests, and Mrs. Wells of providing the conveniences and comforts of her home. The Rev. Genings was given the usual punishment—that he was to be hung, drawn and quartered. Swithin Wells was ordered to suffer a similar martyrdom. While waiting in prison for the sentence to be enforced, he wrote a letter to his brother-in-law, Mr. Gerard Morin. In this letter he explained,

> I have endured much pain, but the many future rewards in the heavenly payment make all pains seem to me a pleasure; and truly custom hath caused that it is now no grief to be debarred from company. . . . I rejoice that thereby I have the better occasion, with prayer, to prepare myself to that happy end for which I was created and placed here by God. . . . yet I am not alone. He is not alone who has Christ in his company. When I pray, I talk with God; when I read, He talketh to me; so that I am never alone. He is my chiefest companion and only comfort.

On the way to the place of execution, which was opposite to Gray's Inn Fields, near the place of his residence, Swithin saw an old friend in the crowd of onlookers and shouted to him, "Farewell, old friend! Farewell all hawking and hunting and old pasttimes—I am now going a better way!"

While Swithin Wells was standing at the scaffold await-ing his execution, the priest-catcher Topcliffe said to him, "See what your priests have brought you to." To this Swithin replied, "I am happy and thank God to have been allowed to have so many and such saint-like priests under my roof."

Swithin Wells was hanged and while still alive was cut

down. When he was being drawn, that is, his viscera and heart were being cut from his body, he cried in agony, but the hangman said later that he heard Swithin invoke the aid of St. Gregory. Also suffering on the same day were priests and other laymen.

Mrs. Wells was also condemned for the same crime, of having harbored priests. She was to suffer the same sentence and was brought to the place of execution. However, after viewing the death of her husband she was remanded to Newgate prison, where she spent ten years in prayer and fasting. She died in prison in 1602. Their daughter, Margaret, eventually became a nun.

Swithin Wells was canonized by Pope Paul VI on October 25, 1970, together with thirty-nine other English martyrs who died between 1535 and 1679.

SIXTY-SIX

SAINT THEODOTA

D. 318

THE Bollandists relate in the *Acta Sanctorum* that Theodota suffered at Plovdiv in Bulgaria, during the year 318.

When Agrippa was persecuting Christians, he commanded that the whole city should join him in offering sacrifice to Apollo during a festival held in the idol's honor. Many in the city complied with the order, but Theodota refused to participate. Previously a harlot, she had converted to Christianity.

When called before the authorities, St. Theodota answered that she had, indeed, been a sinner and would not commit another sin—much less the grievous sacrilege of offering sacrifice to a false god. Her steadfastness encouraged 750 Christians to refuse participation in the sacrifice.

As a punishment for Theodota's disobedience, and because she had been the instrument that influenced so many to offend the god, Theodota was thrown into prison. There she lay for twenty days, praying for courage for herself and her fellow Christians. Called upon once more to answer for her refusal, she again admitted that she had been a harlot and had become a Christian, though she considered herself unworthy to bear that sacred name. Agrippa defiantly ordered that she be scourged.

When those who witnessed her agony urged her to obey the authorities and free herself, Theodota refused. During her scourging she cried, "I will never abandon the true God nor sacrifice to lifeless statues." She was then ordered to be racked and her body torn with an iron comb. Under these tortures, Theodota continued to pray. The judge became enraged at her resolution and ordered that vinegar and salt should be poured into her wounds. When Theodota continued to pray, Agrippa next commanded the executioners to pull out her teeth, which they did with violence. Finally it was ordered that she should be stoned to death.

When she was being led out of the city for her martyrdom, St. Theodota prayed: "O Christ, Who showed favor to Rahab the harlot and received the good thief, turn not Your mercy from me." In this way Theodota died a holy death.

SIXTY-SEVEN

SAINT THOMAS MORE

1478–1535

ST. THOMAS More's father was John More, an attorney, who was so highly respected that he was knighted and made a judge of the Common Pleas. He was later honored as the Justice of the Court of King's Bench. Thomas' mother was Agnes Granger, who died while her son Thomas was still a child. Following his mother's death, Thomas, together with his brother and his two sisters, was placed in the care of a nurse, Mother Maud, whom he fondly remembered later in life.

Following the custom of the time, John More arranged for his son, who was then between twelve and fourteen years old, to serve and be trained in one of the great houses in England. Thomas was fortunate that the place chosen for him was the house of John Morton, archbishop of Canterbury and lord chancellor of England. The Archbishop was also a lawyer and scholar, as well as a diplomat and statesman. Under the Archbishop's guidance, and exposed to countless distinguished guests of the house, Thomas came to appreciate the authority and precepts of the Church and to sympathize with the poor and oppressed. He was also well-trained for public life and won countless friends in important positions.

249

He also developed a natural wit, a kindly tact and an ease at speech-making.

Sometime after Thomas entered Oxford University to study for the bar, he, at sixteen, became greatly infatuated with a young lady who was fourteen. The attraction was mutual, but the girl's parents abruptly ended the matter. Following this first romance, Thomas experienced others. While the ladies seemed to have been attracted to his wit and charm, no scandal was ever lodged against his name.

Erasmus, who became a close friend, wrote of Thomas More, concerning the character of the future saint:

> He seems born and made for friendship, and is a most faithful friend. He so delights in the company and conversation of those whom he likes and trusts, that in this he finds the principal charm of life...Though he is rather too negligent of his own interests, no one is more diligent in those of his friends. . . . He is so kind, so sweet-mannered, that he cheers the dullest spirit and lightens every misfortune. Since his boyhood he has so delighted in merriment that he seems to have been born to make jokes, yet he never carries this to the point of vulgarity, nor has he ever liked bitter pleasantries. If a retort is made against himself, even if it is ill-grounded, he likes it, from the pleasure he finds in witty repartees. He extracts enjoyment from everything, even from things that are most serious. If he converses with the learned and wise, he delights in their talent. . . . With wonderful dexterity he accommodates himself to every disposition. His face is in harmony with his character, being always expressive of a pleasant and friendly cheerfulness and ready to break into smiles. To speak candidly, he is better adapted to merriment than to gravity or dignity, but he is never in the least degree tactless or coarse.

In addition to his law studies, Thomas read Greek philosophy and began to write Latin prose and verse. Concerning these verses, Beatus of Rheinau wrote:

> Thomas More is in every way admirable. How sweetly and easily flow his verses! He writes the purest and clearest Latin, and everything is welded together with so happy a wit that I never read anything with greater pleasure. The Muses must have showered on this man all their gifts of humour, elegance and wit. He jokes, but never with malice, he laughs, but always without offense.

When Thomas began to show a great interest in classical studies, his father became so disappointed that his son was apparently deserting the family's traditional study of the law that he all but disinherited him and almost discontinued his allowance. When this occurred, Erasmus observed that John More was "in other respects a sensible and upright man."

For a time Thomas considered becoming a priest. He also thought of becoming a Franciscan friar or a Carthusian, but then decided upon the married state. To this end he became a welcomed visitor at the country home of Mr. John Colt, who had three daughters. William Roper writes that

> More resorted to the house of one Master Colt, a gentleman of Essex, that had oft invited him thither, having three daughters whose honest conversations and virtuous education provoked him there specially to set his affection. And albeit his mind most served him to the second daughter, for that he thought her the fairest and best favoured, yet when he considered that it would be both great grief and some shame also to the eldest to see her younger sister preferred before her in marriage, he then of a certain pity, framed his fancy toward her and soon after married her.

Erasmus recorded an amusing story, which has been considered on good authority to refer to More and his wife, Jane.

> A young gentleman married a maiden of 17 years who had been educated in the country, and who, being inexperienced, he trusted to form easily in manners to his own humour. He began to instruct her in literature and music and by degrees to repeat the heads of sermons which she heard and generally to acquire the accomplishments he wished her to possess. Used at home to nothing but gossip and play, she at length refused to submit to further training, and when pressed about it threw herself down and beat her head on the ground as though she wished to die.
>
> Her husband concealed his vexation and carried her off for a holiday to her home. Out hunting with his father-in-law, he told his troubles and was urged to "use his authority and beat her!" He replied that he knew his power, but would much rather that she were persuaded, than come to these extremities. The father seized a proper moment, and looking severely on the girl, told her how homely she was, how disagreeable and how lucky to have a husband at all; yet he had found her the best-natured man in the world and she disobeyed him! She returned to her husband and threw herself on the ground, saying: "From this time forward you shall find me a different sort of person!" She kept her resolution and to her dying day, went readily and cheerfully about any duty, however simple, if her husband would have it so.

With the responsibilities of providing for his growing family, Thomas More applied himself to his professional work as a barrister. When defending widows and orphans, he refused all payments. Before long he became known as the most kind, just, skilled and popular attorney in London.

Thomas' home life was happy and prosperous. Little is known of his wife, Jane, except that she was a devoted mother and that she had developed into a delightful companion. But after only six years, Jane died unexpectedly, leaving four surviving children: Margaret, Elizabeth, Cecily and John. For her epitaph, Thomas wrote simply, "Dear Jane lies here, the little wife of Thomas More."

With four children to care for, the eldest being only five years old, Thomas More began almost at once the practical endeavor of finding a stepmother for them. Much to the surprise of his friends, he quickly decided upon a middle-aged widow. Within a few months Thomas married the widow, whom Erasmus describes as "no great beauty, nor yet young, but an active and careful housewife." At this time, More was thirty-four years old; his new wife, Alice Middleton, was seven years older. With the new wife came her daughter, Alice. Later Margaret Giggs joined the household, as did an adopted child, Margaret Clement.

While More acknowledged that Alice was an admirable mother to his children and a careful housekeeper, he accepted with good humor her many shortcomings. Several writers tell us what More had to virtuously contend with. They have described Alice as, "aged, blunt, and rude", "spareful and given to niggardliness" and the "most loquacious, ignorant, and narrow-minded of women."

The virtue of St. Thomas is exemplified in a letter in which he excused his wife's faults in this manner: "I do not think it possible to live even with the best of wives, without some discomfort...this I would say with all the more confidence were it not that generally we make our wives worse by our own faults." On being asked why he chose small women for his wives, he jestingly replied, "If women were necessary evils, was it not wise to choose the smallest evil possible?" More overcame his difficulties with good humor and considerable tact, so that gradually his household became one of joy and comfort. Erasmus wrote:

> He lives with his wife on as sweet and pleasant terms as if she had all the charms of youth...he guides his whole household, in which there are no disturbances or quarrels. If any such arise, he immediately appeases it and sets all right again, never conceiving any enmity himself, nor making an enemy.

Only twice during his lifetime was St. Thomas More known to be angry.

After the publication of More's book, *Utopia,* King Henry VIII prevailed upon Thomas to enter the royal service. More's loyalty and patriotism finally overcame his reluctance, and he resolved to work for the good of his country. More was knighted, and was appointed one of the King's councillors, and then a judge in the Court of Requests, which was otherwise known as the Poor Men's Court. More delighted in this position, since in it he could help the needy in their time of trouble.

Although busy with the court and his duties to the King, More was always mindful of his religious obligations. He wrote that

> delight and pleasure are to be found in spiritual exercises as labour and pain taken in prayer, alms-deeds, pilgrimage, fasting, discipline, tribulation, affliction...The best souls are they that have been travailed in spiritual business, and find most comfort therein.

Thomas More often cautioned his three daughters against

pride and vanity and wrote:

> How delectable is that dainty damsel to the devil that taketh
> herself for fair, weening herself well-liked for her broad fore-
> head, while the young man that beholdeth her, marketh more
> her crooked nose! . . . How proud is many a man over his
> neighbour, because the wool of his gown is finer! And yet as
> fine as it is, a poor sheep ware it on her back before it came
> upon his, and though it be his, is yet not so verily his as it was
> verily hers! . . . All that ever we have, of God we have received;
> riches, royalty, lordship, beauty, strength, learning, wit, body,
> soul and all. And almost all these things hath He but lent us.
> For all these must we depart, except our soul alone.

When members of his family were troubled he would say,
"We may not look at our pleasures to go to Heaven in feath-
erbeds; it is not the way; for Our Lord Himself went thither
with great pain and by many tribulations...The servant may
not look to be in better case than his master."

St. Thomas' home life was well-regulated and a model
of pious living. On Sundays he attended church with all his
household and even when he was Lord Chancellor, he continued to sing in the choir. At night all the family and servants
met together for prayers; at meals, the Scriptures and a short
commentary were read aloud by one of the children.

More had exceptional sympathy for women in labor,
and when he heard that one of the village women was suffering, he would pray until word was brought of her safe
delivery. His charity was boundless. He gave frequently and
abundantly to those in need and would go through back
lanes and inquire about the health and needs of the poor. He
often invited his poorer neighbors to his table and received
them with all respect and gladness. In his parish of Chelsea,

he rented a house in which he gathered the infirm, the poor and the elderly. He maintained all these unfortunates at his own expense.

Another side of More's personality is shown in his hobby of collecting ancient coins and rare books, as well as playing the lute and the viol. Objects of art were kept, not so much because of their value, but more for the quality of the workmanship. Among his treasures was a heart composed of amber in which a fly was imbedded. He likened the fly to friendship, which is kept imprisoned in the heart.

More's interests were turned to more serious matters when King Henry VIII decided to have his marriage to Catherine of Aragon declared null and invalid so that he might marry Anne Boleyn. Wolsey, as lord chancellor of England, visited the Pope on the King's behalf, but failed to obtain the desired annulment. Because of Wolsey's failure in this matter, he was forced to resign. Thomas More was then selected to replace him as lord chancellor.

More accepted the position after he obtained King Henry's promise that he could remain silent on the question of the divorce and remarriage. As chancellor, More was the chief official adviser of the Crown, with functions both administrative and judicial. The Great Seal which he always kept on his person was used to authenticate acts of State and to acknowledge its bearer as the head of the English legal system.

When Henry VIII became infuriated with the Pope over the matter of his divorce, he manipulated Parliament and the House of Lords until finally there was a separation from Rome. Henry VIII then declared that he was the supreme head of the Church of England.

Thomas More was shocked that the King would claim this headship; moreover, he saw the evils to which this claim would lead. With a good conscience, Thomas More refused to acknowledge the King's divorce as being valid and resigned his position as lord chancellor after having served for only two years and seven months. As can be expected, the King was angry with Thomas for not agreeing with him, but he delayed his revenge for another time.

The loss of his office reduced More's income to a small pension. Having been generous to the poor, he was left with no savings on which to rely, nor did he own valuable property. In one aspect only was he favored, as he wrote to Erasmus:

> From the time of my boyhood, dearest Desiderius, I have longed that I might someday enjoy what I rejoice in your having always enjoyed—namely, that being free from public business, I might have some time to devote to God, prayer and myself. This, by the grace of a good God, and by the favour of an indulgent prince, I have at last obtained.

On March 30, 1534, the Act of Supremacy was enacted. It provided for the taking of an oath by all the King's subjects in which they acknowledged that his union with Catherine of Aragon had been an invalid marriage, that the King's union with Anne Boleyn was valid and that their offspring would be the legitimate heirs to the throne. The taking of the oath also involved the repudiation of "any foreign authority, prince or potentate." A refusal to take the oath was considered to be high treason. Many Catholics took the oath with the reservation, "so far as it be not contrary to the law of God."

When those who opposed the King were charged with treason and were imprisoned and beheaded, Thomas More knew that his time would also come. On April 12, 1534, he was ordered to appear before the commissioners for the purpose of taking the new oath. The next day the saint attended Holy Mass, confessed and departed from his home for the last time. On appearing before the Commission, Thomas More refused to accept a repudiation of papal authority in England or to take the oath under any condition. The Commission gave him time to reconsider, but he did not change his mind. Therefore he was committed to the Tower.

At first the jailers treated the saint with some leniency, permitting him visits from his beloved daughter, Margaret, and his wife. He was permitted to correspond with his friends, but later he was deprived of his chief consolation, his books and papers. His wife did not understand her husband's decision and wanted him to return home. Margaret tried to persuade her father to take the oath, but Thomas stood firm, gently calling her "Mother Eve" for her efforts to tempt him.

After fifteen months of harsh imprisonment, Thomas' health was greatly impaired. Looking older than his fifty-eight years, he was brought to stand trial on July 1, 1535. At the Bar of the Court of King's Bench, in Westminster Hall, Thomas was charged with high treason and with maliciously attempting to deprive the King of his title of supreme head of the Church of England.

It is said that Thomas More could not defend the personal qualities of the popes of his time, who were often openly criticized, but Thomas could not deny that the Pope was the visible head of the entire Church.

The guilty verdict was expected. Weeping at this time was Sir William Kingston, constable of the Tower, who was

Thomas' friend. William Roper, Thomas' son-in-law, wrote of this scene:

> There with a heavy heart, the tears running down his cheeks, William Kingston bade him farewell. Sir Thomas More, seeing him so sorrowful, comforted him with as good words as he could, saying "Good Master Kingston, trouble not yourself, but be of good cheer for I will pray for you and my good lady your wife, that we may meet in Heaven together, where we shall be merry for ever and ever."

Also meeting him with tearful farewells were members of his family.

The day before he died, the future saint sent to his beloved daughter, Margaret, the hair shirt he had worn for many years as a penance. This he attempted to give her in secret, not wanting his wife, or others, to know of it.

Early in the morning of July 6, 1535, word was brought to the saint that he was to be beheaded before nine o'clock. He thanked the messenger for his "good tidings" and remarked that he was most of all "bounded to his highness that it pleaseth him so shortly to rid me out of the miseries of this wretched world."

Upon arriving at the scaffold, his physical weakness was apparent when he asked for help in words that have become famous, "I pray you, Master Lieutenant, see me safe up; as for my coming down, let me shift for myself." After speaking a few words to the people, he asked for their prayers and begged them to pray to God for the King. He added, "I call you to witness, brothers, that I die in and for the Faith of the Catholic Church; the King's loyal servant, but God's first." After More encouraged the headsman, his head was placed on the block. He arranged his beard so that it would not be touched by the axe, saying, "For it at least had committed no treason."

The body of the saint was interred for a time in the little chapel of St. Peter ad Vincula in the Tower. His head was exposed on a stake on London Bridge, where it remained for almost a month before his daughter, Margaret Roper, was able to claim it.

In the Anglican church of St. Dunstan, in Canterbury, Kent, is found the St. Nicholas or Roper Chapel. A marble slab located there informs the visitor that "beneath this floor is the vault of the Roper family in which is interred the head of Sir Thomas More." When the marble was placed on the floor of the chapel in 1932, the head of the saint was believed to be in the vault. However, in 1978, which marked the five hundredth anniversary of the birth of Thomas More, an archaeological survey of the chapel was undertaken. This revealed that the skull of St. Thomas More was found "in a leaden casket in a niche in the North Wall."

Like St. Thomas Becket before him, who was chancellor of England and keeper of the Great Seal, Thomas More also died for the doctrine of the Church by means of the blade. But unlike Thomas Becket, who was an archbishop, Thomas More was a layman, and an exemplary husband and father. Another difference between the two is that while Thomas Becket was canonized soon after his death, Thomas More had to wait four hundred years, until 1935, to gain this distinction. In recent years, the lives of both saints were portrayed in award-winning motion pictures: Thomas Becket in *Becket*, and Thomas More in *A Man for All Seasons*.

SIXTY-EIGHT

BLESSED THOMAS PERCY

D. 1572

WHEN Thomas Percy's father died a martyr at Tyburn for having denied the ecclesiastical supremacy of King Henry VIII, his two children, Thomas and Henry, were forcibly removed from the care of their mother, who was named "treasonable." They were placed in a number of foster homes, including that of Sir Thomas Tempest of Tong. In 1549, when Thomas came of age, the attainder under which he and Henry had suffered as a result of their father's actions was, to a certain extent, removed. They were "restored in blood," and shortly thereafter Thomas was knighted.

Three years later, during Queen Mary's reign, he regained his ancestral honors and lands. After being named governor of Prudhoe Castle, Thomas Percy besieged and took Scarborough Castle from the rebel, Sir Thomas Stafford. This so pleased Queen Mary that she named Thomas Percy the earl of Northumberland—an earldom to which his martyred father had been heir-presumptive. This title was given Thomas in consideration of his "noble descent, constancy in virtue, valour in arms, and other strong qualifications." Also given him at that time were the Baronies of Percy, Fitzpane, Plynings, Lucy and Bryan. He was installed at Whitehall with great pomp and soon was named Warden General of the Marches. In this capacity he served the Queen well in military and civil affairs on the Scottish border.

In 1558 he married Anne Somerset, daughter of the Earl of Worcester. She is described as a valiant woman who subsequently suffered much for the Faith.

After Elizabeth ascended the throne and was passing anti-Catholic measures in Parliament and laying the foundations of the Anglican Church, Thomas, who was known to be steadfastly loyal to the Catholic Church, was in the north, safely out of the turmoil. But for reasons not given, he soon resigned the wardenship and moved to the south. Queen Elizabeth favored the Earl and in 1563 gave him the Order of the Garter. When he was in the north, he played only a minor part in opposing the Queen and did so with considerable prudence. His lack of action and his acceptance of the Order of the Garter made him later express his dissatisfaction with his own behavior.

The north of England was still solidly Catholic. A Protestant observer said of Yorkshire that, "There were scarcely ten gentlemen of note that favour the Queen's proceedings in religion," and when Mary, Queen of Scots had to take refuge at Carlisle in 1568, she was soon regarded as the Catholic champion.

The following year—with the systematic persecution of the Catholics—those in the north, anticipating the excommunication of Elizabeth, were planning a campaign to liberate Queen Mary. The organizers of this rebellion were of the opinion that Mary should be the next heir to the throne so that she could "restore the Crown, the nobility, and the worship of God to their former estate."

Thomas had some misgivings about the project and made it clear that it was not a political endeavor, saying, "We are seeking, I imagine, the glory not of men but of God." He agreed to participate in the liberation, "to have some reformation in religion, or at the least some sufferance for men to use their conscience as they were disposed."

Thomas Percy, with the Earl of Westmoreland, wrote to Pope Pius V asking for advice; but before an answer was received from Rome, circumstances rushed them into action, against their better judgment. Their plan had become known to the authorities, and the two earls were summoned to appear before Elizabeth. A hasty meeting of the leaders was called at Brancepeth Castle. Although Thomas Percy disagreed, it was decided that the earls should ignore the summons. Instead, on November 14, the two earls marched into Durham at the head of their forces. The villagers welcomed them enthusiastically, and the cathedral was immediately restored to Catholic worship. Under the supervision of the Reverend William Holmes, altars were restored and decorated, and Protestant prayerbooks were destroyed.

On St. Andrew's feast day, High Mass was sung in the cathedral, and on the following Sunday the Reverend Holmes publicly reconciled the huge congregation. After eleven years of forced apostasy, the people joyously greeted the celebration of Holy Mass. Under the banner depicting the Five Holy Wounds, Thomas Percy, with Bl. Thomas Plumtree as chief chaplain, marched into Yorkshire and Wetherby, collecting recruits and encouraging the people. They turned again to the north, where they captured Hartlepool and Barnard Castle.

This, however, was the limit of their success. At the end of a month, Elizabeth's troops, under the Earl of Sussex, forced the earls to see the futility of further combat. Thomas Percy and the Earl of Westmoreland sadly disbanded their men at Durham, and fled across the border into Scotland.

The Earl of Sussex took revenge on the people who had reverted to the public celebration of their faith, and hanged them by the hundreds. Escaping punishment was Thomas Percy's wife, who was one of the leading forces of the rebellion. She eventually came under the protection of Lord Home and died in exile at Namur.

Thomas Percy was captured by the Scottish regent, the Earl of Moray, and was imprisoned in Lochleven Castle for two and a half years while negotiations for his sale to the English government were being conducted. Dr. Nicholas Sander, a leading Catholic of the day, records that Thomas Percy bore his imprisonment and separation from his four small children and his wife with great patience. Thomas Percy, he wrote, observed all the fasts of the Church, spent a great deal of time in prayer and meditation, wrote a book of prayers which still exists, and emphatically refused an offer that he deny his faith in order to gain his pardon.

He was conducted to York and was lodged in the castle on August 21, 1572. He was offered a last chance to win his freedom on condition of apostasy, but he again refused. After being told he would die the next day, he spent all night in prayer. The next afternoon he was taken to the scaffold, where he told the people that he died a Catholic: "As for this new Church of England, I do not acknowledge it." He expressed sorrow that he had occasioned the death of so many as the result of the aborted rebellion, saying, "Yet I have no fear but that their souls have obtained the glory of Heaven." Following these words he was beheaded—to the sorrow of many, because "throughout his life he was beyond measure dear to the whole people." He was forty-four years old. Thomas Percy was beatified with other English martyrs by Leo XIII in 1896.

His daughter Mary Percy founded the Benedictine convent at Brussels, from which nearly all the existing houses of Benedictine nuns in England are descended.

SIXTY-NINE

BLESSED THOMAS SHERWOOD

D. 1578

B ECAUSE we have contemporary documents, as well as an account of the life of Thomas Sherwood that was written by his brother, we are well-informed concerning the life and death of this twenty-seven-year-old martyr. His father was Henry Sherwood, a woolen draper (a maker or dealer in cloth). His mother was Elizabeth, who in thirty years of marriage gave birth to fourteen children.

Thomas Sherwood was born in London and was well-instructed in the Catholic faith by his two devout parents. He attended school until his fifteenth year, when he was removed to help in his father's cloth business. In the *Acts of English Martyrs,* Pollen tells us that Thomas was

> of small learning, scarcely understanding the Latin tongue, but had much read books of controversies and devotion, and had used much to converse among Catholic priests, and by reason thereof, having a good wit and judgment, and withal being very devout and religious, he was able to give good counsel, as he did to many of the more ignorant sort, being much esteemed for his virtuous life and humble and modest behaviour: besides, God did give a special grace in his conversation, whereby together with his good example of life,

he much moved and edified others. He was a man of little stature of body, yet of a healthful and good constitution, and very temperate in his diet.

After helping his father for a few years, Thomas felt himself called to the religious life. Because adherents to the Roman Catholic Church were being persecuted in England by Queen Elizabeth, Thomas Sherwood's parents permitted him to "pass the seas" to the seminary at Douai, France. Told by the priests that he must resume his studies, Thomas traveled back to London to make financial arrangements for his support and tuition.

One morning, while walking down Chancery Lane in London, he met George Martin, the son of Lady Tregonwell (also Tregony). George Martin had seen Thomas many times at his mother's house in the company of a priest who was known as Mr. Stampe. Challoner suggests that George Martin resented Sherwood, believing that Mass was sometimes privately celebrated in his mother's home, and that Thomas Sherwood was arranging these meetings that placed his mother in jeopardy.

On seeing Thomas that morning, George Martin called for the constable and had his former friend arrested. While Thomas was standing before Mr. Fleetwood, the recorder of London, George Martin testified that Sherwood was often in the company of priests and that he had even traveled across the seas to confer with traitors. The Recorder then asked Thomas what he thought of the Bull of Pius V and whether, if the Pope had excommunicated the Queen, she was then the lawful queen or not.

To this Sherwood answered according to his conscience, saying that if the Pope had indeed excommunicated the Queen, then he thought she could not be the lawful monarch—that he did not believe the Queen to be the head of the Church of England, and that this preeminence belonged to the Pope.

As to other questions asked of him regarding his journey to Douai, he would not answer. Having been betrayed by one whom he thought was a friend, Sherwood was committed to the Tower of London, where he was confined in a dark cell near the torture chamber. As soon as he was locked away, his lodgings were searched and plundered of all that he had, including money he had borrowed for the use of his father.

During the early days of his confinement, he was harassed and tortured in the hope that he would confess where he had heard Mass, or reveal the names of priests who were conducting these unlawful services. He was racked twice, but refused to answer any questions. As a result of the tortures, he lost the use of his legs. He was left without necessary clothing and was thrown into a filthy dungeon where his jailers thought the darkness, the stench, an insufficient amount of food and his nakedness would break his will.

Word of his sad condition reached Mr. Roper, the son-in-law of St. Thomas More, who offered the young prisoner some money for food. When the jailers refused to let their prisoner have the money, they did permit Mr. Roper to buy sixpence of straw for Thomas Sherwood to lie on.

In his book entitled *Torture in the Criminal Law of England,* Mr. Jardine gives us a description of the cell in which Thomas was confined:

The cell was below high water mark and totally dark. As the tide flowed, innumerable rats, which infest the muddy banks of the Thames, were driven through the orifices of the walls into the dungeon. The alarm excited by the irruption of these loathsome creatures in the dark was the least part of the torture which the unfortunate captives had to undergo; instances are related, which humanity would gladly believe to be the exaggerations of Catholic partisans, where the flesh had been torn from the arms and legs of prisoners during sleep by the well-known voracity of these animals.

After a time the prisoner was interrogated by the Privy Council and by Gilbert Gerard, the attorney general. Thomas Sherwood repeated the same statement he had made to the Recorder, that if the Queen had been excommunicated, then she could not be the lawful queen of England. What then occurred is given in the letter of the Lords of the Privy Council which reveals that the Lieutenant of the Tower and others were "to assay him (Sherwood) at the rack upon such articles as they shall think meet to minister unto him for discovering either of the persons or of further matters." That is, they wanted to obtain information that would convict other Catholics—information that Thomas Sherwood refused to give them even under severe torture.

Six months after his apprehension, Thomas was brought to trial. Part of the official record of his trial from the *Coram Rege Roll* (20 Eliz. rot. 3) reads as follows:

Otherwise, to wit, in the term of St. Michael last part, before our Lady the Queen at Westminster, by the oath of 12 jurors, it was presented that Thomas Sherwood, late of London, yeoman, on the 20th of November, in the 20th year of the Lady Elizabeth, by the grace of God Queen of England, France and

Ireland, Defender of the Faith . . . in the city of Westminster in the County of Middlesex, diabolically, maliciously, and traitorously, compassing, imagining, thinking, devising, and intending the deprivation and deposition of the said Lady Queen Elizabeth, from her style honour, and royal title to the imperial crown of this kingdom of England, did, out of his own perverse and treacherous mind and imagination, maliciously, expressly, advisedly, directly and traitorously . . . say these false English words . . . to wit that "for so much as our Queen Elizabeth doth expressly disassent in Religion from the Catholic Faith, of which Catholic Faith, he sayeth that the Pope Gregory the Thirteenth that now is, is conserver, because he is God's General Vicar in earth: and therefore he affirmeth by express words that our said Queen Elizabeth is a schismatic and an heretic," to the very great scandal and derogation of the person of our Lady the Queen.

The court records reveal the end of the trial in this manner:

The jury, therefore, then came before our Lady the Queen at Westminster, on Monday, the morrow of the Purification of Blessed Mary the Virgin...on which day Thomas Sherwood in his own proper person came before our Lady the Queen... under ward of the Lieutenant. The Sheriff returned the names of 12 jurymen, which jurymen having been impanelled and summoned for this, came to say truth about and over the premises. Who, having been elected, tried and sworn, say upon their oath that the aforesaid Thomas Sherwood is guilty of the several high treasons laid against him. Also that the self-same Thomas Sherwood hath no goods or chattels, land or tenements to their knowledge.

When the prisoner was asked if he could say anything for himself why the court should not proceed judgment and execution of the verdict, Thomas "sayeth no otherwise than as he said above." The Attorney General, Gilbert Gerald, then ordered that

Thomas Sherwood be led by the aforesaid Lieutenant unto the Tower of London, and thence be dragged through the midst of the City of London, directly unto the gallows of Tyburn, and upon the gallows there be hanged, and thrown living to the earth, and that his bowels be taken from his belly, and whilst he is alive be burnt, and that his head be cut off, and that his body be divided into four parts, and that his head and quarters be placed where our Lady the Queen please to assign them.

No one has preserved for us the details of Sherwood's conduct at the place of execution, but three weeks later, news of the death of this martyr reached the seminary at Douai. In the records of the seminary this notation is found:

On the first of March (1578), Mr. Lowe returned to us from England, bringing news that a youth, by name (Thomas) Sherwood, had suffered for his confession of the Catholic Faith, not only imprisonment, but death itself. Amidst all his torments his exclamation had been, "Lord Jesus, I am not worthy to suffer this for Thee, much less to receive those rewards which Thou hast promised to those that confess Thee."

Having courageously endured a cruel imprisonment, chains, hunger, cold, stench, nakedness and the rack, Thomas Sherwood won the martyr's crown at Tyburn, London, on February 7, 1578, being only twenty-seven years of age.

SEVENTY

SAINT VICTOR OF MARSEILLES

D. 304

WHEN Emperor Maximian arrived at Marseilles, France, the flourishing Christian community became fearful of the persecution that was imminent. Victor, as a Christian officer in the Roman army, went secretly at night to the homes of the faithful, inspiring them with contempt of a temporal death and the love of eternal life.

After a time, his activities were discovered by the authorities, who ordered his arrest and arraignment before the prefects. These attempted to win him over to their pagan beliefs by telling him that he was serving Jesus Christ who was no more than a dead man, and that his promotion in the army and the favor of high authorities were at risk by this allegiance to a false religion.

Victor confronted his accusers by declaring that Jesus Christ was the Son of the true God, that He rose from the dead and reigns at God's right hand. The assembly responded to the words with shouts of rage, but because of Victor's high rank, the prefects did not know what punishment was appropriate and sent him to Maximian for sentencing.

The Emperor attempted to win him over with kindness,

but when this failed, imprisonment and punishment were threatened. This, too, had no effect on Victor, who remained constant in his beliefs. Maximian at length commanded that Victor be bound hand and foot and dragged through the streets of the city, thinking that he would not only punish Victor, but that this would also serve as a warning and lesson to other Christians. The Emperor's treatment of Victor, and the saint's courage during this trial, had an opposite effect, and only served to encourage the faithful.

Bruised and bloody from his ordeal, Victor was ordered to adore the Roman gods, but he refused and expressed his contempt for the gods and his love for Jesus Christ. One of the prefects, Asterius, then commanded him to be hoisted on a rack, on which he was stretched for a lengthy time. When Victor was finally taken down, he was thrown into a dungeon. But then a wonderful thing took place. At midnight Victor was visited by his Savior, who was accompanied by angels. The prison was filled with a bright light, while heavenly voices were heard praising God. Three guards of the prison saw the light, and upon seeing the vision, fell to their knees and were instantly converted to the Faith. Their names are given as Alexander, Longinus and Felician. That same night they were secretly baptized.

Eventually Maximian learned about the conversion of the guards, and in a fury he ordered that they be beheaded. Encouraged during their last moments by Victor, the three soldiers were martyred while confessing their belief in Jesus Christ. Victor was tortured for his part in the conversion of the guards and was once again brought before the Emperor. He was commanded to offer sacrifice and to incense a statue of Jupiter, but Victor showed his contempt for the false god by kicking it with his foot. As punishment for this insult to Jupiter, Victor's foot was promptly chopped off by order of the Emperor. Victor was then sentenced to be crushed to death, but when this did not end his life, he was decapitated. The year was 304.

The bodies of the four martyrs were thrown into the sea, but were recovered by Christians who gave them a proper burial. Both St. Gregory of Tours and Venantius Fortunatus recorded that the tomb of St. Victor at Marseilles was one of the best-known places of pilgrimage on French soil. In the fifth century, the Benedictines at Marseilles erected an abbey above the tomb of the martyrs. But, at the time of the Revolution of 1793, the relics were either misplaced or destroyed.

SEVENTY-ONE

SAINT WERNHER

D. 1275

HIS AGE is not given, but St. Wernher is known to have been a child when he was abducted by non-Christians. Their purpose was to obtain possession of the Blessed Sacrament, or, at least, to use the blood of a Christian child for their magical or cultist rites.

It is believed that Wernher was seized after receiving Holy Communion on Maundy Thursday in the year 1275. He was hung by the heels in the hope that he would disgorge the wafer he had swallowed. When this failed, he was killed. His blood was drained before his body was carelessly thrown into a pit at Bacherach. When the boy's remains were discovered, the murderers were seized and executed for the crime.

Wernher was buried at Trier, where miracles soon occurred at his tomb. His feast was celebrated throughout Germany, but especially in the City of Trier, where the death of the little martyr was remembered with great sadness.

SEVENTY-TWO

BLESSED WILLIAM HOWARD

1614–1680

DIRECTLY descended from distinguished representa-
tives of religion and art, Bl. William claims as his
grandfather St. Philip Howard, the earl of Arundel, who died
in prison for the Faith in 1595. St. Philip's son, Thomas,
who was born while his father was in prison, is recognized as
the first great art collector of England and the father of our
Bl. William Howard.

Born on November 30, 1614, William was educated in
the Catholic faith, and by the age of fourteen he was made a
Knight of the Bath at the coronation of King Charles I. When
he was twenty-three years old, he secretly married Mary
Stafford, the Catholic sister of the last Baron Stafford. Soon
afterward King Charles raised him to the rank of viscount.

Recognized as a loyal supporter of the King, William
was entrusted by both Charles and Emperor Ferdinand with
responsible assignments on the continent, where he, like his
father, indulged in the collection of fine art.

Upon the death of his father in 1646, William was
thrust into a prolonged dispute with his eldest surviving
brother, Earl Henry Frederick, over what remained of their

inheritance. The Howard properties in England had been seized by Parliament, which greatly impoverished the family. This prompted Earl Henry Frederick to commence a series of unjust and vexing civil suits against his mother, during which he almost succeeded in robbing her of her dowry.

William, as her representative and defender, was involved in painful quarrels even after both mother and brother had passed away. His cousins and their agents continued against him for several years over the issue, which William continued as a matter of principle. In 1655, lawsuits were pending in Douai, Brussels and Amsterdam. While William fought for what was just and proper against scheming relatives who were vindictive and greedy, he was to be defended by his Benedictine confessor, Dom Maurus Corker, who wrote that William was "ever held to be of a generous disposition, very charitable, devout, addicted to sobriety, inoffensive in his words and a lover of justice."

In addition to court battles with his relatives, William had other troubles—these being literary friends of his father who were claiming manuscripts and rarities from the Arundel Collections. William successfully defended the collection, which created bitter enemies of the defeated claimants. They wrote bitter complaints against William, which found a permanent place in the diaries and works of distinguished writers.

When his lands were restored to William in 1660, "He lived in peace, plenty, and happiness, being blessed with a most virtuous lady to his wife, and many pious and dutiful children, in which state he remained till the sixty-sixth year of his age."

In 1678, Titus Oates created a false claim called the

Popish Plot, in which he alleged that Catholics planned to assassinate Charles II, land a French army in England and turn the government over to the Jesuits. The House of Commons apparently believed the tale, since countless Catholics were martyred as traitors to the Crown. Lord Stafford was included in the list of suspects who were supposed to have sided with the Pope against the English nation. It is believed that William was named because his age, simplicity and the previous differences with members of his family would make it comparatively easy to obtain a conviction.

On October 25, William was taken to the King's Bench Prison. From there he was transferred with others to the Tower. Two years elapsed before he was taken to trial. When he did appear before the House of Lords, who had assembled in Westminster Hall, the prosecutor's witnesses were such scoundrels as Dugdale, the Irish ex-Dominican Dennis, the apostate priest Smith, Tuberville and Oates himself. William Howard, being now in his late sixties, was somewhat deaf and could not properly hear all that the perjurers testified against him, yet Challoner writes that

> these managers with all imaginable art and malice baited the good old gentleman for four whole days...but such was the force of truth and innocence and so good was his defense (notwithstanding the great fatigue of so many days' pleading and all the eloquence employed against him), and brought such and so just exceptions against the witnesses and such proofs of their being perjured villains, that every unprejudiced man that will but read the memoirs of his trial, must agree that he was very unjustly condemned. However, such was the iniquity of the times and the aversion to his religion, he was found guilty by 55 lords and acquitted only by 31.

When the votes were counted and William was pronounced guilty of high treason, he replied, "God's Holy Name be praised for it. I confess I am surprised at it, for I did not expect it. But God's will be done, and your lordship's. I will not murmur at it. God forgive those who have falsely sworn against me."

After the Lord High Steward delivered an abusive speech against Catholics, William was sentenced to be hung, drawn and quartered. The King, however, disapproved of both the verdict and the sentence, but was successful only in changing the manner of execution (to beheading).

Dom Maurus Corker, Bl. William's confessor and fellow prisoner, wrote that William spent the three weeks before his execution "in serious reflection and fervent prayer, wherein he seemed to find a daily increase of courage and of comfort, as if the Divine Goodness intended to ripen him for martyrdom and give him a foretaste of Heaven."

William wrote his testament, of which several drafts are extant. In these he denied the charges against him by writing, "I hold the murder of one's sovereign a greater sin than anything since the Passion of our Saviour." He also wrote in moving terms of his grief, and his willingness to leave, for the sake of God, his "most deserving wife and most dutiful children... Receive, therefore, most dear Jesus, this voluntary oblation." He wrote to his children, and before dressing on the day of his death, he wrote a tender and loving letter to his wife.

On December 19, 1680, the day of William's death, several thousand people crowded on Tower Hill to witness the execution. Some are said to have paid a guinea for a favorable position.

After mounting the scaffold, William declared his innocence and expressed the opinion that he was being charged because of his religion. After praying aloud, he delivered a long discourse in which he professed his faith in all that the Catholic Church teaches. He exhorted all to pledge allegiance to their king in civil matters, and to give support to the Pope in matters of religion. He begged God to bless the crowd and to forgive his false accusers, as well as the executioner, who is identified as Jack Ketch. William Howard then kissed the block. He made the Sign of the Cross, and commended himself to the Divine Mercy before he adjusted his head for the axe. At the sight of the elderly gentleman being unjustly executed, many in the crowd took pity on him and called aloud for God to bless him.

Bl. William Howard was sixty-six years old at the time of his death on December 19, 1680. It was only in 1824 that Bl. William's title was awarded to Sir George William Stafford Jerningham, who became the eighth Lord Stafford. In 1929, Pope Pius XI beatified William Howard as a true martyr of the Church.

SEVENTY-THREE

SAINT WILLIAM
OF NORWICH

1132–1144

WILLIAM, the son of Wenstan and Elviva, was born on Candlemas Day, probably in the year 1132, and was baptized in Haveringland Church. At the age of eight he began to learn the trade of a tanner, and in a few years he was employed in Norwich, England, where furs were in great demand for clothing and coverlets. William's trade brought him to the attention of wealthy Jews who lived under the King's protection near Norwich Castle. This district is now bounded by White Lion Street and the Haymarket. William made friends among the Jews, and although such mixed friendships were not unknown, they were unusual since the Jews were somewhat distrusted and generally only grudgingly tolerated by the Christians. For reasons not given, it seems that with the approach of the Lenten season in the year 1144, William's uncle forbade his association with his Jewish friends. This might have caused apprehension or resentment within the Jewish community.

For the remaining history of St. William of Norwich we are indebted to Thomas of Monmouth, who became a monk of the cathedral priory of Norwich. He investigated the matter and wrote the details of the murder of William in the second book of his *Vita en Passio*.

Thomas of Monmouth tells us that on Monday in Holy Week in the year 1144, William, who was then twelve years old, was lured away from his mother by someone who offered him employment in the Archdeacon's household. A relative of the boy became suspicious of the whole story and followed William and his companion until he saw them enter the house of a Jew. William was never seen alive again.

The events that next transpired were later revealed by Jewish converts to Christianity and a servant of the house. Their accounts reveal that on Wednesday in Holy Week, after a service in the synagogue, the Jews meant to mock the Crucifixion, in contempt of Christ. They lacerated William's head with thorns, crucified him and pierced his side. On Holy Saturday, the twenty-fifth of March, Aelward Ded witnessed the Jew, Eleazar, and another man carrying a heavy sack to Mousehold, a wooded area near Norwich. When the sack was discovered a few hours later, it revealed William's mutilated body, which bore the clear signs of a violent death.

When word reached the Jewish community that the body had been found, they immediately went to the castle and placed themselves under the protection of the sheriff, who is said to have received a large bribe to guard them. The move was merely an act of prudence, since the boy's mother and relatives soon accused the Jews of the crime.

On Easter Monday the body was temporarily buried where it lay at Mousehold, and visits were frequently made there by young men and boys who had known the victim. A few days later the priest Godwin Sturt, William's uncle, formally accused the Jews at the Bishop's synod and then had the grave opened; the body was recognized as that of William.

Because of the nature of the wounds and the season of the year in which the Crucifixion had been re-enacted on the boy, the guilt of the Jews seemed confirmed. Since the Jews were then the King's men and under the protection of the sheriff, the Bishop, who had also brought charges, had no jurisdiction in the case. A number of bribes were known to have been offered to various individuals to suppress the story or drop the charges in the case. The only result was that the body of the boy martyr was removed on April 24 from Mousehold to the monks' cemetery at the cathedral.

When Aelward Ded, who had discovered the body of the boy in the sack, was on his deathbed five years later, he told what he knew of the crime. As a result, Thomas of Monmouth, the monk chronicler, interviewed a Christian serving-woman who was employed in the house where the crime had been committed. She told how she had peered through a crack in a door and had caught sight of a boy fastened to a post. She had been ordered to bring hot water to her master, presumably to cleanse the body. She afterward found a boy's belt in the room and showed Thomas of Monmouth the marks of the martyrdom that were found in the room. Despite the evidence and the eye-witnesses, no one seems to have been brought to justice for the crime.

Due to the reports of miracles worked through the boy martyr's intercession, William of Turbeville, bishop of Norwich (1146-1174), on four different occasions had the boy's remains transferred to more honorable places. The last transfer was to the Martyr's Chapel (now the Jesus Chapel) in

Norwich Cathedral. Unfortunately, no trace of St. William's shrine remains, although its site is still known. In 1168, the Bishop erected a chapel in the woods where William's body had been discovered. The site of this chapel can still be visited.

Elias, prior of the cathedral (1146-1150), and some of the monks at first were skeptical about the miracles. However, the doubts of skeptics were overcome when miracles continued to take place, and when several monks had premonitory visions or dreams.

The boy from Haveringland became St. William, martyr, with a feast day on March 24.

INDEX OF SAINTS
THEIR LIVES AND DIFFICULTIES

I T IS our prayer that this Index will be helpful to the lay members of the Church who are trying to live in a truly Christian manner while confronted by the many difficulties and temptations of the world. May these laymen draw courage and determination to endure or overcome their difficulties by examining the lives of the secular saints who also experienced countless trials, but who bravely surmounted them by turning to God and trusting in His holy will. Those who are enduring a particular trial or temptation can discover those saints who experienced a somewhat similar problem by examining the appropriate category of the Index, which is divided thus:

I   Married Saints
       Married Men
       Married Women
II   Widows and Widowers
III Unmarried Saints
IV Parenting
V   Childhood
VI Deaths of the Saints
       Murder

An apology might be made to those saints whose faults or sins are featured here. Since these are given with the sole intention of offering an example that might encourage the layman to overcome his difficulties and to advance in virtue, the saints will, undoubtedly, excuse the exposure of their failings.

Through the Communion of Saints, we can claim these holy people as our blessed friends in heaven. May they pray for us that we will profit by their example so that we, too, may overcome the dangers of this world and merit to join them someday in our heavenly homeland.

I.   MARRIED SAINTS

Married Saints: Bl. Adrian Fortescue; St. Anne Lyne; St. Aurelius; Bl. Charles the Good; St. Edwin; St. Hermengild; Bl. James Duckett; St. James Intercisus; St. Julitta; St. Margaret Clitherow; Bl. Margaret Pole; St. Margaret Ward; St. Perpetua; St. Polyeuctus; Bl. Ralph Milner; St. Richard Gwyn; Bl. Richard Herst; St. Swithin Wells; St. Thomas More; Bl. Thomas Percy; Bl. William Howard.

MARRIED MEN

Bad-Tempered or Nagging Wife: St. Thomas More.
Disappointed in Love (loved one but married another): St. Thomas More.

MARRIED WOMEN

Childless: St. Anne Lyne.

Vow of Virginity Made before Marriage that Was Respected after Marriage: St. Cecilia.

II. WIDOWS AND WIDOWERS

Widows: St. Anne Lyne; St. Felicitas; St. Julitta.

Widowers: Bl. Adrian Fortescue; St. Edwin; St. Thomas More.

Saints Who Married Widows: Bl. James Duckett; St. Thomas More.

Widows Who Raised Children Alone: Bl. Margaret Pole.

Widowers Who Remarried: Bl. Adrian Fortescue; St. Edwin; St. Thomas More.

III. UNMARRIED SAINTS

Bachelor Saints: St. Boniface of Tarsus; Bl. Edward Coleman; St. Epipodius; St. John Rigby; Bl. Marcel Callo; St. Serenus; Bl. Thomas Sherwood.

Unmarried Women Saints: St. Agatha; St. Bibiana; St. Flora; St. Julitta; St. Nunilo; Bl. Pierina Morosini.

Vow Of Chastity or Virginity Made by Unmarried Saints: St. Agatha; St. Nunilo; Bl. Pierina Morosini; St. Serenus.

IV. PARENTING

Mothers of Large Families (5 children or more): St. Felicitas, 7; Bl. Margaret Pole, 5.

Mothers (1-4 children): St. Felicitas, 1; St. Julitta, 1; St. Margaret Clitherow, 3; St. Perpetua, 1.

Fathers of Large Families (5 children or more): Bl. Adrian Fortescue, 5; St. Edwin, 6; Bl. Ralph Milner, 7; St. Richard
Gwyn, 6; Bl. Richard Herst, 7.

Fathers (1-4 children): St. Hermengild, 1; Bl. James Duckett,
1; Bl. John Felton, 2; St. Polyeuctus; St. Swithin Wells,
1; St. Thomas More, 4; Bl. Thomas Percy, 4; Bl. William
Howard.

Adopted Children (saints who adopted): St. Thomas More.

Death of Children: St. Felicitas, 1 child; St. Felicitas, 7 sons
martyred; St. Julitta, 1 son; St. Perpetua, 1 child.

Difficulty with Parents (saints who had problems with their
parents): St. Hermengild; St. Regina.

Gave Birth in Prison: St. Felicitas.

Saints Who Were Stepparents: St. Thomas More.

Saints Who Had Stepparents: St. Hermengild.

Saints Who Had Trouble with Stepparents: St. Hermengild;
Sts. Nunilo and Alodia.

V. CHILDHOOD

Child Abuse (saints who experienced abuse during their
childhood): St. Alodia; St. Nunilo.

Died Young: St. Agnes, 12; Bl. Antonia Mesina, 16;
St. Dymphna, 15; St. Eulalia, 12; St. Hallvard, adoles-
cent; Bl. James Bird, 19; Bl. Margaret of Louvain, 18;
St. Regina, 15; St. Simon of Trent, 2; St. Solangia;
St. Wernher; St. William of Norwich, 12.

Foster Homes (saints who lived in foster homes): St. Edwin;
Bl. Thomas Percy.

Kidnapped Children: St. Simon of Trent; St. Wernher;
St. William of Norwich.

Orphaned: St. Aurelius.

Poor Circumstances (some saints who grew up in poor surroundings): Bl. Antonia Mesina; St. Solangia.

Ran Away from Home: St. Alodia; St. Dymphna; St. Eulalia; St. Nunilo.

Removed from Parents: Bl. Thomas Percy.

Responsibilities When Young: Bl. Antonia Mesina; Bl. Pierina Morosini.

VI. DEATHS OF THE SAINTS

Betrayed by Friend: Bl. James Duckett; Bl. Thomas Sherwood.

Betrayed by Relatives: St. Flora, brother.

Betrayed by Servant: St. Alexander; St. Epipodius.

Died for Purity: St. Agatha; St. Agnes; Bl. Antonia Mesina; St. Dymphna; Bl. Pierina Morosini; St. Potamiana; St. Solangia.

Died in Prison From Sickness: Bl. Marcel Callo.

Gave Life for Another: St. Alban; St. Hallvard; St. Margaret Ward.

Imprisoned for a Time before Martyrdom: Bl. Adrian Fortescue; St. Alexander; St. Agatha; St. Agnes; St. Alodia; Bl. Edward Coleman; St. Epipodius; St. Felicitas; Bl. Flora; St. Hermengild; Bl. James Duckett; Bl. John Bodey; Bl. John Felton; St. John Rigby; Bl. John Slade; Bl. Marcel Callo; St. Margaret Clitherow; Bl. Margaret Pole; St. Margaret Ward; St. Mary; Ven. Nicholas Horner; St. Nunilo; St. Perpetua; St. Polyeuctus; Bl. Ralph Milner; St. Regina; St. Richard Gwyn; Bl. Richard Herst; St. Swithin Wells; St. Thomas More; Bl. Thomas

Percy; Bl. Thomas Sherwood; St. Victor of Marseilles; Bl. William Howard.

Killed in Battle: St. Edwin.

MURDER

Murder Attempted against Saints: St. Edwin.

Saints Who Were Murdered: Bl. Charles the Good; Bl. Margaret of Louvain.

Saints Murdered by Relatives: St. Dymphna, father; St. Hermengild, father.

Murdered by Students: St. Cassian.

Tortured (some of the saints who were tortured before dying): St. Agatha; St. Alban; St. Alexander; St. Anthony; St. Bibiana; St. Blandina; St. Charles Lwanga and Companions; St. Edmund; St. Epipodius; St. Eulalia of Merida; St. Eustace; St. Genesius; St. James Intercisus; St. John; Bl. John Felton; St. John Rigby; St. Julia; St. Julitta; St. Margaret Ward; Ven. Nicholas Horner; St. Pantaleon; St. Regina; St. Richard Gwyn; St. Sabas; St. Simon of Trent; St. Theodota; Bl. Thomas Sherwood; St. Victor of Marseilles; St. William of Norwich.

VII. GENERAL

Abandoned: St. Flora.

Accused Wrongfully: St. Blandina; Bl. Edward Coleman; Bl. Margaret Pole; Bl. Richard Herst; St. Serenus; Bl. William Howard.

Cared for Incapacitated Relative: Bl. Antonia Mesina, cared for her mother.

Converts: St. Afra; St. Alban; St. Anne Lyne; St. Boniface

of Tarsus; St. Charles Lwanga and Companions;
Bl. Edward Coleman; St. Edwin; St. Flora; St. Genesius;
St. Hermengild; Bl. James Bird; Bl. James Duckett;
St. Lucian; St. Margaret Clitherow; St. Philemon;
Bl. Ralph Milner; St. Theodota.

Court (saints who were brought before the court for a civil
matter): St. Julitta; Bl. William Howard.

Forced to Leave Home (for various reasons): St. Anne Lyne;
St. Edwin; St. Flora; Bl. Marcel Callo; St. Regina.

Homelessness (some of the saints who experienced homelessness for various lengths of time): St. Edwin.

Illiterate: Bl. Ralph Milner.

Kidnapped Adult. Bl. Margaret of Louvain was killed during
kidnapping.

Left the Faith and Later Returned: St. James Intercisus;
St. Pantaleon.

Formally Renounced the Faith and Later Returned: St. James
Intercisus.

Saint Who Endured Another's Mental Disability:
St. Dymphna.

Mistakes (some of the saints who made grave or foolish mistakes): St. Hermengild; Bl. Thomas Percy.

Neglected (some of the saints who experienced this):
St. Edwin.

Nursing the Sick (some of the saints who attended the sick):
St. Pantaleon.

Black Magic: St. Lucian and St. Marcian.

Fire Worshippers: Sts. Anthony, Eustace and John.

Penitents: St. Afra; Bl. Boniface of Tarsus; St. John Rigby; St. Theodota.

Personality Outgoing And Likeable: Bl. Marcel Callo.

Poor (some of the saints who helped the poor): Bl. Charles the Good; Sts. Cosmas and Damian; St. Thomas More.

Poverty (saints who lived in poverty or were reduced to poverty): St. Regina.

Rape Victim: Bl. Pierina Morosini.

Rejection (some of the saints who experienced rejection): St. Edwin; St. Regina.

Sick and Handicapped Saints: Ven. Nicholas Horner, amputated leg.

TERTIARIES

Dominican: Bl. Adrian Fortescue.

TROUBLE WITH FAMILY MEMBERS

Trouble with Fathers: St. Dymphna; St. Hermengild; St. Regina.

Trouble with Brothers: St. Flora.

Trouble with An Aunt: Bl. Charles the Good.

Trouble with Cousins: Bl. William Howard.

Trouble with A Stepmother: St. Hermengild.

Trouble with A Stepfather: St. Nunilo and St. Alodia.

Unfair Actions Experienced by Saints (some of the saints who were deprived of property, money or position): St. Anne Lyne; St. Bibiana; St. Edwin; St. Hermengild; St. Julia; St. Julitta; Bl. Margaret Pole; Bl. Thomas Percy; Bl. Thomas Sherwood; Bl. William Howard.

VIII. OCCUPATIONS AND HOBBIES

Art Collector: Bl. William Howard.

Attorneys: St. Thomas More.

Business Woman: St. Margaret Clitherow.

Butcher Shop (worked in): St. Margaret Clitherow.

Centurion: St. Marcellus.

Cloth Dealer: Bl. Thomas Sherwood.

Comedian: St. Genesius.

Country Gentleman: Bl. Adrian Fortescue.

Counts: Bl. Charles the Good.

Crusaders: Bl. Charles the Good.

Dancer: St. Philemon.

Farmers: Bl. Ralph Milner; Bl. Richard Herst.

Gardener: St. Serenus.

Governess: Bl. Margaret Pole.

Housewives: St. Anne Lyne; St. Margaret Clitherow.

Hunters: St. Swithin Wells; St. Thomas More.

Innkeepers: St. Anne Lyne; Bl. Margaret of Louvain.

Justice of the Peace: Bl. Adrian Fortescue.

Kings: St. Edmund; St. Edwin.

Knights: Bl. Charles the Good.

Leader of Rebellion: Bl. Thomas Percy.

Lectors: St. Sabas.

Lord Chancellor of England: St. Thomas More.

Merchants: St. Hallvard.

Mill Worker: Bl. Pierina Morosini.

Musicians: St. Philemon.

Occultists (before conversion): Sts. John, Anthony and
    Eustace; St. Lucian and St. Marcian.

Physicians: Sts. Cosmas and Damian; St. Pantaleon.

Prostitutes (before conversion): St. Afra.

Princesses: St. Dymphna.

Prisoners (worked with): St. Margaret Ward; Bl. Ralph Milner.

Publisher (dealer of books): Bl. James Duckett.

Roman Officers: St. Polyeuctus; St. Victor of Marseilles.

Scholars: Bl. John Bodey; St. Richard Gwyn.

Secretary: Bl. Edward Coleman.

Servants: St. John Rigby.

Sewing: Bl. Pierina Morosini.

Shepherdesses: St. Regina; St. Solangia.

Shoemakers: Bl. Anthony Primaldi.

Slaves: St. Blandina; St. Felicitas; St. Julia; St. Potamiana.

Soldiers: St. Edwin; St. Hermengild; St. James Intercisus.

Tailor: Ven. Nicholas Horner.

Tanner's Assistant: St. William of Norwich.

Teachers: St. Cassian; Bl. John Slade; St. Richard Gwyn; St. Swithin Wells.

Waitress: Bl. Margaret of Louvain.

Writers: St. Thomas More.

BIBLIOGRAPHY

Albertson, S.J., Clinton. *Anglo-Saxon Saints and Heroes.* Fordham University Press. Bronx, New York. 1967.

Albin, The Rev. Hugh O. *The Parish Church of St. Dunstan.* Canterbury, Kent, England.

Arnold, Anneliese. *Hospice Built on Hallowed Ground,* Rochester, England. (Paper.)

Aston, Margaret. *The Fifteenth Century.* Harcourt, Brace & World, Inc. London. 1968.

Attwater, Donald. *Saints of the East.* P. J. Kenedy & Sons. New York. 1963.

Attwater. *Martyrs from St. Stephen to John Tung.* Sheed & Ward. New York. 1957.

Ball, Ann. *Modern Saints—Their Lives and Faces.* TAN Books & Publishers, Inc. Rockford, Illinois. 1983.

Basil the Great, St. *Letters.* Volume II. Fathers of the Church, Inc. New York. 1955.

Beda Venerabilis. *The Ecclesiastical History of the English Nation.* J.M. Dent & Sons, Ltd. London, England. 1958.

Benedictine Monks of St. Augustine's Abbey, Ramsgate. *The Book of Saints.* Thomas Y. Crowell Company. New York. 1966.

Bouin, Rev. Paul. *The Uganda Martyrs.* The Regina Press. Turnhout, Belgium. 1965.

Brewer, E. Cobham. *A Dictionary of Miracles.* Cassell & Company, Ltd. New York. 1884.

Butler, Alban; Thurston, S.J., Herbert; Attwater, Donald. *The Lives of the Saints.* 12 Volumes. P. J. Kenedy & Sons. New York. 1934.

Butler, N. V. Pierce. *A Book of British Saints.* The Faith Press, Ltd. London, England. 1957.

Camm, O.S.B., Dom Bede. *Forgotten Shrines.* MacDonald & Evans. London, England. 1936.

Caraman, S.J., Philip. *Margaret Clitherow.* The Catholic Truth Society. London, England. 1986.

The Catholic Encyclopedia. The Encyclopedia Press, Inc. New York. 1909.

Challoner, D.D., Richard. *Memoirs of Missionary Priests.* Burns, Oates and Washbourne, Ltd. London, England. 1924.

Chapter of St. Albans Cathedral. *A Visit to St. Albans Cathedral.* St. Albans, England. 1984.

Chioccioni, T.O.R.; P. Pietro. *Illustrated Guide to the Basilica of Saints Cosmas & Damian.* The Basilica of Saints Cosmas and Damian. Rome, Italy. 1973.

Clarke, James Freeman. *Events and Epochs in Religious History.* James R. Osgood & Co. Boston. 1883.

Colledge, O.S.B., Edmund; Walsh, S.J., James. *Following the Saints.* Good Will Publishers, Inc. Gastonia, North Carolina. 1970.

Conyngham, D. P. *Lives of the Irish Saints and Martyrs.* P. J. Kenedy & Sons. New York. 1870.

Coulton, G. G. *Life in the Middle Ages.* Cambridge University Press. London. 1967.

Cruz, Joan Carroll. *The Incorruptibles.* TAN Books and Publishers, Inc. Rockford, Illinois. 1977.

Cruz. *Relics.* Our Sunday Visitor, Inc. Huntington, Indiana. 1983.

Dahmus. *The Middle Ages.* Doubleday & Co., Inc. Garden City, New York. 1968.

De Bruges, Galbert. *Le Meurtre De Charles Le Bon,* Fonds Mercator-*Anvers. Antwerp, Belgium. 1987.*

de Grunwald, Constantin. *Saints of Russia.* Hutchinson of London. London, England. 1960.

Delehaye, Hippolyte. *The Legends of the Saints.* Fordham University Press. New York. 1962.

De Liguori, St. Alphonsus. *The Way of Salvation and of Perfection.* Redemptorist Fathers. Brooklyn, New York. 1926.

De Liguori, St. Alphonsus. *Victories of the Martyrs.* Redemptorist Fathers. Brooklyn, New York. 1935.

de Sales, St. Francis. *Introduction to the Devout Life.* Harper & Brothers, Publishers. New York. 1950.

Dickens, A. G. *The English Reformation.* Schocken Books, New York. 1964.

Drane, Augusta Theodosia. *The Life of St. Dominic.* Burns & Oates, Ltd. New York. 1919.

Eglise Fortifiee De Hunawihr. Edite par l'Association des Amis de l'Eglise Historique de Hunawihr. Alsace.

Englebert, Omer. *The Lives of the Saints.* Translated by Christopher and Anne Fremantle. Collier Books. New York. 1964.

Eusebius. *The Ecclesiastical History.* William Heinemann, Ltd. London. 1926.

Fathers of the Church, Funeral Orations by St. Gregory Nazianzen and St. Ambrose. Volume 22. Fathers of the Church, Inc. New York. 1953.

Fathers of the Church, St. Basil Ascetical Works. Catholic University of America Press. Washington, D.C. 1962.

Favrais, Robert; Royer, Eugene. *Marcel Callo, Jociste et Martyr.* Supplement of Actualites Notre Temps. Coutances, France. August-September 1987.

Gostling, Frances M. *The Lure of English Cathedrals.* Robert M. McBride & Co. New York. 1926.

Gregory the Great, St. *The Dialogues of S. Gregorie.* The Scholar Press. London, England. 1975.

Gueranger, Rev. Prosper. *Life of Saint Cecilia, Virgin and Martyr.* Peter F. Cunningham. Philadelphia.

Hartman, C.SS.R., Rev. Louis F., Editor. *Lives of Saints.* John J. Crawley & Co., Inc. New York. 1962.

Hieronymus, Saint Jerome. *Select Letters of St. Jerome.* William Heinemann, Ltd. London. 1933.

Iswolsky, Helene. *Christ in Russia.* The Bruce Publishing Co. Milwaukee. 1960.

Jones, Charles W. *Saints' Lives and Chronicles in Early England.* Cornell University Press. Ithaca, New York. 1947.

Karel de Goede, 1127-1977. Onthalcentrum. Brugge, Belgium. 1977.

Lamb, Harold. *The Crusades.* Doubleday & Co., Inc. Garden City, New York. 1931.

Larsen, Karen. *A History of Norway.* Princeton University Press. Princeton, New Jersey. 1948.

Larsson, Raymond E. *Saints at Prayer.* Coward-McCann, Inc. New York. 1942.

Lettere. *Nella Gloria Del Bernini.* Periodico Bimestrale della Causa di Beatifieazione di Papa Giovanni e Pierini Morosini. November-December, 1987.

Lettere. *Pierina Morosini. Giovane Laica Martire.* Periodico Bimestrale della Causa di Beatificazione di Papa Giovanni e Pierina Morosini. Settembre-Ottobre, 1987.

Loades, D. M. *The Oxford Martyrs.* Stein and Day Publishers. New York. 1970.

L'Ortobene. Edizione Speciale. Nuoro, Italy. September 27, 1987. (Newspaper article.)

Macken, Rev. Thomas F. *The Canonisation of Saints.* M. H. Gill & Son, Ltd. Dublin. 1910.

Mann, Rev. Horace K. *The Lives of the Popes in the Early Middle Ages.* Volume V. Kegan, Paul, Trench, Trubner & Co., Ltd. London. 1925.

Mann. *The Lives of the Popes in the Middle Ages.* Volume XI. Kegan, Paul, Trench, Trubner & Co., Ltd. London. 1925.

Marion, Francis. *New African Saints.* Ancora Publishers. Milan, Italy. 1964.

Melis, Mons. Giovanni. *Antonia Mesina Sugli Altari.* Editrice Stamperia Artistica-Sassari. Italy. 1987.

Murphy, S.S.J., Rev. Edward F. *Hand Clasps with the Holy.* Society of the Divine Saviour Publishing Dept. St. Hazianz, Wisconsin. 1941.

Neligan, Rev. William H. *Saintly Characters Recently Presented for Canonization.* P. J. Kenedy & Co. New York. 1859.

Newland, Mary Reed. *The Saints and Our Children*. P. J. Kenedy & Sons. New York. 1958.

O'Connell, Canon J. B., Editor. *The Roman Martyrology*. The Newman Press. Westminster, Maryland. 1962.

Pamphili, Eusebius. *The Ecclesiastical History*. Fathers of the Church. Catholic University of America Press. Washington, D.C. Volumes I and II. 1955.

Passionista, P. Fortunato. *La Beata Antonia Mesina*. Nettuno, Italy. 1987.

Pollen, John Hungerford. *Acts of English Martyrs*. Burns and Oates, Ltd. London. 1891.

Pope, Mrs. *The Lives of the Early Martyrs*. D. & J. Sadlier & Co. New York. 1856.

Previte-Orton, C. W. *The Shorter Cambridge Medieval History*. Cambridge University Press. Cambridge, Great Britain. 1971.

Riasanovsky, Nicholas V. *A History of Russia*. Oxford University Press. London. 1969.

Routh, E.M.G. *Sir Thomas More and His Friends, 1477-1535*. Oxford University Press. London, England. 1934.

Sanna, Giovanni. *Martirio a Orgosolo, Antonia Mesina*. Editrice L'Ortobene, Nuoro, Italy. 1987.

Sharp, Mary. *A Guide to the Churches of Rome*. Chilton Books. New York. 1966.

Stenton, Sir Frank M. *Anglo-Saxon England*. Oxford University Press. London, England. 1943.

Stevenson, J., Editor. *A New Eusebius*. The Macmillan Company. New York. 1957.

Terzi, Ignazio. *Le Due Corone-Verginita e Martirio in Pierina Morosini*. Edizione Instituto Grafico Litostampa.

Coordinazione a cura dell'Opera Barbarigo. Bergamo, Italy. 1984.

Trigg, Joseph Wilson. *Origen.* John Knox Press. Atlanta. 1983.

Undset, Sigrid. *Saga of Saints.* Longmans, Green & Co. New York. 1934.

White, Helen C. *Tudor Book of Saints and Martyrs.* The University of Wisconsin Press. Madison, Wisconsin. 1963.

William of Norwich, (1132-1144.) Cathedral of Norwich. (Paper.)

Yonge, Charles Duke. *The Seven Heroines of Christendom.* W. Swan Sonnenschein & Co. London. 1883.